Millesvik
Norwich
Skibbereen
Polotsk
Berlin
Bisacquino
Hacienda Buenavista
Gold Coast

Picture Credits

The Bettmann Archive, Inc.: pp. 11, 55, 62, 65, 66, 75, 78, 81, 85, 88, 178; Historical Pictures Service, Chicago: pp. 48–49, 110, 164, 174; Hutchinson Publishing Group Ltd.: pp. 151, 154; New York Public Library, Astor, Lenox and Tilden Foundations: p. 41; Photo Researchers, Inc.: photo by E. Boubat—pp. 140–141, 143, 148–149, photo by Harry Crosby—pp. 192, 199, photo by Fritz Henle—p. 191, photo by John Stage—p. 187; Picture Collection, New York Public Library, Astor, Lenox and Tilden Foundations: pp. 2–3, 14, 28, 50, 97, 126, 188; reprinted by permission of G. P. Putnam's Sons from *Life in Stuart England* by Maurice Ashley, copyright © 1964 by Maurice Ashley: p. 5; Swedish Information Service: pp. 122–123; Lionel S. Reiss, *My Models Were Jews—A Painter's Pilgrimage to Many Lands*, The Gordon Press, 1938: pp. 167, 172.

Harbrace map

Curriculum-Related Books, selected and edited by the School Department of Harcourt, Brace & World, are titles of general interest for individual reading.

Library of Congress Catalog Card Number: 69-11493

Printed in the United States of America

First edition

TO AMERICA

Eleanor B. Tripp

HARCOURT, BRACE & WORLD, INC., NEW YORK

ACKNOWLEDGMENTS

While writing this book I have had the help of many people. I am grateful to the librarians and staff of the American-Irish Historical Society, the American Jewish Committee, the YIVO Institute for Jewish Research, and the New York Public Library for their assistance in my research.

It is a pleasure to acknowledge those who read the various chapters critically and corrected errors of fact and interpretation: Chapter 1—Jean S. Wilson of Smith College; Chapter 2—Carol Kellogg of the Shady Hill School, Marion D. de B. Kilson of the University of Massachusetts; Chapter 3—Catherine E. O'Driscoll, James E. O'Driscoll; Chapter 4—Hanns G. Reissner of the New York Institute of Technology at Old Westbury and Queens College; Chapter 5—Myron L. Cohen of Columbia University; Chapter 6—Gerhardt T. Rooth, editor-publisher of *The Swedish North Star;* Chapter 7—Rev. Joseph A. Cogo, C.S., of the American Committee on Italian Migration, Rev. Silvano M. Tomasi, C.S., of the *International Migration Review;* Chapter 8—Lucy S. Dawidowicz of the American Jewish Committee, Sherwin M. Goldman; and Chapter 9—Marvin D. Bernstein of the State University College at Fredonia, New York and Charles C. Cumberland of Michigan State University.

I also want to thank Steven M. L. Aronson, Anne Janeway, Dorothy M. Miner, and Robert S. November for their help. My brother, James T. B. Tripp, offered indispensable assistance and encouragement throughout my work on the book. I alone accept responsibility for any errors that remain.

Eleanor B. Tripp
NEW YORK CITY, JULY 2, 1968

For my Mother and Father

FOREWORD

Books that deal with immigration to America often focus on the lures that inspired people to strike out for a new life and the adjustments that transplanted families made in the United States. Rather than describing primarily what was pulling emigrants toward a new home, this book concentrates on what was pushing them from the old. Each of the nine chapters details life in a specific community at a time of significant emigration from the country of which that community was a part. From these accounts emerges a sense of the impact of overpopulation, industrialization, internal strife, oppression, and the poverty of an unchanging peasant life on the people of those various towns and villages. Despite those pressures, each emigrant made a free choice to leave his native land with the exception of the African, who forsook his home only when he was taken away by physical force. Roughly speaking, the nine communities represent the origins of the largest immigrant groups in the history of the United States. Because of space limitations, it has been impossible to include a chapter on every major immigrant group. Therefore, an attempt has been made to select groups that present the widest possible range of conditions motivating emigration.

CONTENTS

Foreword vii

FROM AUTHORITY
Norwich, England, 1630's 1

FROM FREEDOM
The African Gold Coast, 1731 25

FROM FAMINE
Skibbereen, Ireland, 1845-1848 47

FROM TYRANNY
Berlin, Prussia, 1848-1849 72

FROM DISORDER
En-p'ing, China, 1860's 96

FROM LANDLESSNESS
Millesvik, Sweden, 1880's 119

FROM FUTILITY
Bisacquino, Sicily, 1900-1910 139

FROM OPPRESSION
Polotsk, Russia, 1900-1914 162

FROM PEONAGE
Hacienda Buenavista, Mexico, 1920's 184

Immigration Facts and Figures 203

Reference Notes 210

FROM AUTHORITY

Norwich, England, 1630's

A DIVIDED TOWN

Along the high road running inland from Yarmouth on the North Sea, the green fields of the rolling countryside looked fertile and ready to produce healthy crops of rye and wheat. Sheep grazing on the land promised a good supply of wool for spinning and weaving into cloth. The river Yare looped into the walled town of Norwich where a great stone castle and the lofty spire of a cathedral rose above the closely built, tile-roofed houses that sheltered the twelve thousand people who lived in England's third largest town. Its market place and narrow streets, flanked by craftsmen's shops, were filled with traders and shopkeepers, servants and housewives, wool buyers and yeoman farmers, rich merchants and poor beggars. Norwich looked busy and prosperous, but the spire of the cathedral, casting a shadow on the market streets below, symbolized only one of the many troubles brewing.

Although everyone in town had been born into the

Norwich's clustered houses, its fortress and cathedral,

can be seen in this view from across the river Yare.

same Anglican, or English, Church, about half the inhabitants disagreed with the other half as to how it should be run. As it stood, the king controlled the church and wanted to keep the worship the way it was; those who agreed with him were called Anglicans. The other half wanted more control of the church for themselves, and they wanted to change the style of worship; some of these people, though technically Anglicans, were called Puritans. A number of others who might not have thought of themselves as Puritans, at least shared certain Puritan ideas. Whether or not a man liked the king's religion, he took his family on Sunday mornings to the church nearest home, which might be the cathedral itself or one of the thirty parish churches within or beyond the town walls. (According to law, every Englishman was required to attend his neighborhood church and risked paying a fine if he were absent.) In church, Puritans sat in pews beside Anglicans who were happy enough with the king and his religion, opened the same Prayer Book, and read the same Bible. Yet when Anglicans and Puritans met in a tavern they often engaged in heated debate. On Sunday afternoons, taunting words or even blows were sometimes exchanged on the village greens.

Most Englishmen liked to spend the afternoon that followed a six-day work-week dancing, wrestling, bowling, and playing football (like our soccer) on the greens. In contrast, Puritans felt the entire Sabbath should be devoted to God and good works. When brightly dressed Anglicans were sporting on the grass, they were often annoyed by shouts from Puritans standing at the sidelines in unfashionable dark clothes, or startled by the

A dark-garbed Puritan minister and two Puritans at prayer.

onrush as Puritans ran across the field to break up the games.

The soberest Puritans dressed in gray or brown wool jerkins and dark wool or leather breeches with black stockings. They wore ruffs around their necks, an effect which had gone out of style some years earlier, or flat white collars and pointed shoes, also out of date. Other Englishmen, in contrast, donned orange or purple jerkins, red or blue breeches, and equally bright stockings. At their necks, they usually wore elaborate lace collars and their shoes were quite fashionably blunt-toed. The wives of the rich wore large feather hats instead of the dark, loose-fitting hoods worn by Puritan women.

Puritans thought a good deal about the next life, the life in heaven or hell to follow the life on earth. Most Puritans assumed God had chosen them to go to heaven, but they could never be sure. Although leading an industrious and pious life would not get them into heaven if God had decided otherwise, the fact that a man wanted to lead such a life would show that he was among the godly. Each household said prayers together, morning and evening. Puritans read and studied the Bible; they puzzled out for themselves the meanings of its stories and passages; they took to heart the warnings God had given in the past against the extravagance of kings and their courts, and against such laziness, drunkenness, and gambling as could be seen around them in Norwich. They valued industriousness and thrift and worked long hours at their businesses. They visited the sick, gave money to charity and, even in the cold of winter evenings, walked to extra prayer meetings. At night, many would record in diaries their thoughts on religion, and examine their closeness to God.

Anglicans, on the other hand, did not spend much time thinking about God and the next life. They read their Bibles but seldom mused over hidden meanings. Believing that God had selected them for heaven or hell long before, Anglicans relaxed in the pleasures of life without feeling guilty or sinful. Anglican shopkeepers who had taken in a bit of money by noon were known to close their shutters early and enjoy the rest of the afternoon outdoors or in a tavern, and day laborers loitered about the village alehouse when the yeoman who had hired them was not around.

During church services, Puritan ministers wore simple black robes, refusing to don the elegant white surplice that most Anglican ministers wore. They did not read word for word from the Prayer Book as other ministers did, but left out the phrases that displeased them and sometimes even made up their own prayers. As the high point of the service, they delivered their own sermons. Anglican ministers always lighted candles on the altar and bowed at every mention of the name of Jesus Christ; they seldom gave sermons, following instead the colorful ritual and ceremony of former days. Speaking in flowery set phrases, they added little of their own to the traditional service. These clergymen insisted that church members kneel to pray, exchange wedding rings at their marriages, and allow the sign of the cross to be made over their children at baptism. They loved just such vestments, ritual, and ceremony as the Puritans despised: "The Ceremonies and apparell tend not to edification, but destruction," the Puritans said, "no man by them is directed to Christ and the sincerities of the Gospell."[1]

Such questions as whether or not to wear a surplice or bow at the mention of Jesus were part of a long-standing debate that was still taking place all over Europe. Reformers were trying to simplify their Roman Catholic worship to the pure spiritual form they believed Jesus Christ would have wanted. As a result, various Protestant denominations had grown out of the Catholicism that had been Europe's religion for centuries.

A hundred years earlier, in the reign of Henry VIII, Parliament had broken all ties with the pope in Rome and transferred the English church to Henry's control. Monasteries were gutted and their windows broken; the Catholic worship of relics was discontinued. Under

[1] Reference notes for quotations will be found, listed by chapter, on pages 210-214.

Henry's son, Edward VI, other changes came about. Crucifixes and statues of saints, stained-glass windows and religious paintings were removed from the churches; holy water was no longer used; ministers were allowed to marry. More and more of the service was conducted in English instead of Latin, and the English Prayer Book, setting down the mode of worship, was adopted in all churches. But the king held onto the old church organization of archbishops and bishops, and to the idea of a set form of service.

Extreme Puritans demanded that the reform go further, to the point where each parish governed itself without bishops. This worried Charles I, who was king in the 1630's, for he knew that only through the bishops could he control the religious life of his subjects. Fearful of having the church undermined, King Charles ordered his Puritan subjects to cease trying to change its organization or its service. For this, all the Puritans of Norwich hated the king. In Norwich, the clergy, gentry, merchants, and middlemen inclined toward Puritanism, while the craftsmen and yeomen were divided between Puritan and Anglican sympathies. Bishop Corbet, who owed his position in Norwich to the king, remained loyal to Anglicanism as did the nobles who were appointed to important posts by Charles, and who enjoyed the pleasures of his court in London. The day laborers, servants, and paupers, who made up nearly half the population of Norwich, ignored the controversy but generally favored the king's religion. Few people in Norwich maintained a true enthusiasm for Charles, however; they tended to blame him for a number of secular dissatisfactions.

VOICES OF COMPLAINT

The richest men in Norwich were merchants who traded with cities distant from England. They belonged to companies that sent ships laden with English cloth and grain across the Channel to Europe or with English settlers across the Atlantic to Virginia and the Massachusetts Bay Colony. Other ships might return to the wharves in London or Yarmouth with tobacco from Virginia, furs from Russia, lemons from Portugal, wines from France, copper from Germany, and tea and silks from the Orient. A select group of Norwich merchants sat together on the town council, which met in the guild hall near the market place in the center of town.

The men with the most prestige were not these merchants, but the gentry, whose two-story manor houses were the largest in the countryside. These men owned entire villages, or nearly so, and they leased to yeomen the land they did not farm themselves. During the winter months, the gentry frequently rented houses in Norwich, where they socialized with the richer merchants.

Settled outside the town walls, where there was less crowding and a lower chance of fires and epidemics, gentry and merchants exchanged hospitality in the paneled rooms of their four-storied town houses. Visitors, who entered through a carved doorway, were seated on hand-carved and upholstered chairs and served elegant meals, such as goose and artichokes, on expensive dishes at places set with fine silverware. Usually they drank chocolate or coffee, but in the richest houses tea from China was poured. Despite this luxury, the conversation at the table was frequently full of dissatisfaction. The rich complained of heavy taxes and criticized King Charles for dismissing at his whim the Parliament elected by Englishmen of property.

A few years earlier, a number of Englishmen in Parliament had thought the king's officials incompetent and extravagant; they thought, too, that the king had no right to call an end to reform in the Church of England. To try to control the king, they had refused to vote the money he needed for his personal and national expenses and, in anger, Charles dismissed Parliament. Throughout the 1630's, he never called it back. Without its vote he could not levy general taxes, so he sidestepped Parliament by expanding an old right of special wartime taxation. In the past, the king had been allowed to tax seaport towns for money to build ships for defense in time of war. Now, in peacetime, he was collecting a ship tax from everyone in England who owned property on the pretext that the nation might be drawn into religious wars being fought on the continent. The gentry and the rich merchants turned over their taxes grudgingly, and Charles spent the money as he chose. People feared that if the king kept on collecting ship money he would never have to call Parliament again.

The gentry and merchants were not the only property owners affected by the ship tax. Immediately below them on the status scale came the merchants we would call middlemen today—wool brokers, grain dealers, and clothiers. The clothiers were especially successful, since Norwich was the center of England's two-hundred-year-old business of manufacturing and trading woolen cloth. Waiting for their cloth to be checked for defects and

This seventeenth-century poster illustrates the importance of the wool industry to the economy of England.

put up for sale in the cloth hall, clothiers were heard to remark unhappily about the burden of the new tax and about the long-drawn-out wars on the continent that were cutting them off from their European markets. Markets everywhere, in Antwerp and Amsterdam as well as in Norwich, Yarmouth, and London, were important to the clothier.

On Wednesdays and Saturdays, the established market days, clothiers would hasten to the market place in Norwich to buy sheared wool from the yeomen who had carried it in from the surrounding countryside, or from traveling wool dealers who had carted it south from Lincolnshire. The clothier would turn his newly purchased shearings over to carders, combers, and spinners. These craftsmen, working long hours for piece wages, transformed the raw sheep's wool into yarn in their own cottages. The clothier took the spun yarn and passed it on to weavers who wove it into cloth. This was turned over to fullers and dyers. Dozens of men, women, and children might work at home in their cottages on each batch of wool before the finished cloth was wound neatly into bolts and returned to the clothier. He sold the bolts to merchants who loaded them onto pack horses and set out on a high road that ran southward through Ipswich to London and the market there. A few years earlier, he would have shipped a good number of bolts to the continent and sold them off in European cities and towns. Now that the wars had closed these markets, the clothiers were beginning to feel the pinch of lowered incomes, though they still fared better than the craftsmen.

An ornate sign marked the shop of each craftsman in

the streets and narrow lanes where the wooden houses of shoemakers, tailors, or hatters were located. Walking through the front door, a customer came to a counter where he could inspect the craftsman's handiwork. After making a purchase, he would often lean on the counter and chat about current troubles, such as Charles's latest threat to the Puritans or rumors that an epidemic of plague was on its way to Norwich. The craftsman, perhaps a hat maker, might reply that the Puritans should leave well enough alone, and that there was nothing to be done about the epidemic since it was God's way of punishing men for their sins. Handing the hat to his customer, he would turn to inspect the bolts of felt brought into his shop by a felt dealer who wanted to show his goods to the craftsman and his apprentices. At the end of the day, a craftsman went up to the rooms above his shop where he lived with his family and his apprentices. He sat down to a meal of bread and cheese—or beef, bacon, and mutton when the budget allowed—and vegetables from his wife's garden behind the house. He and his apprentices sometimes discussed the ever-present danger of being pushed out of business by the king.

In exchange for a substantial sum of money, King Charles would grant a group of men the sole right to carry out a process vital to a certain craft. For example, nobles belonging to his court would buy a monopoly on the dying of wool draperies. Dyers of wool draperies in Norwich and everywhere else would be out of luck and lose their trade. Craftsmen thrown out of business by monopolies spoke with hatred against the king.

Although equal in status to a craftsman, a farmer, or yeoman, lived in more spacious surroundings. His stone or half-timbered house stood amidst fields and gardens, all of which he rented from the gentry. The roof of the house was made of thatch and the windows fit only loosely, making the rooms drafty and cold. The house had neither running water nor drains. A paid water carrier brought water regularly, and in some small, dark room a large bucket served as a privy.

Handmade oak tables and benches, chairs and chests in the main hall and other rooms were brightened with woven fabrics. At noontime, the yeoman's wife spread

Much activity takes place outside a yeoman's house.

a cloth over the long narrow table in the hall and laid out a few spoons and knives. She marked each place with a large linen napkin, important for wiping fingers that became greasy from holding pieces of mutton. She pickled boar's flesh to make brawn, pig's feet to make souse, churned butter, pressed cheese, baked bread, and brewed beer to serve her family. An old ballad sang:

Talk not of goose and capon,
give me good beef and bacon,
And good bread and cheese now at hand:
With pudding, brawn and souse,
all in a farmer's house,
That is living for the husbandman.[2]

Aside from preparing food, the wife and her daughters carded wool, spun it on the wheels found in every yeoman's household, took the yarn to a weaver in Norwich, and later cut and sewed the finished cloth into clothing for the family.

On Wednesday and Saturday mornings, the yeomen and their wives carried or carted extra butter and cheese, fruits and vegetables into the open square in the center of Norwich. Tramping the dusty country roads on their way to market, yeomen looked with concern at their neighbors' farms and sheep. Heavy rains the last few years had caused poor harvests. The yeomen looked to see how the new crop was prospering, and they could not fail to observe that there was less land planted than in the years past. Many a pasture that had once been sown with rye was now grazed by sheep. The grandfathers of these yeomen had found they could earn more money from shorn wool than they could from rye or wheat. Gradually, more sheep appeared in the meadows. Lately, this practice of investing in sheep had proved disastrous, since the wet seasons had brought sheep rot, a dreaded liver ailment that killed many of the animals. Times were bad for the yeomen; they worried about having the money to pay the gentry for their leases in order to keep them to pass on to their oldest sons. Even in the best years it was only the oldest son who inherited his father's place on the family farm. The younger boys were apprenticed to craftsmen, traders, merchants, or ship captains in Norwich.

The yeomen reached the walls of the town and joined others in setting out produce. Housewives and servants from Norwich moved quickly among them comparing prices. Around them, they heard the cries of weavers selling cloth, butchers buying animals for slaughter, brokers from Lincolnshire selling wool, and dealers from London buying grain. When the market closed for the day, yeomen and traders would head for the nearest tavern. Over a pint of ale, a zealous Puritan yeoman would turn an idle conversation with a saddler or blacksmith into a lively debate. He might begin by suggesting that a certain country gentleman should give the vacant house and farmland of a retiring Anglican minister to a young cleric of Puritan persuasion. From this discussion, the yeomen would work up to far more abstract topics such as who was destined for heaven, the need to purify the church, or the value of allowing every word of the Bible to direct daily life. If the remarks grew too heated, friends might intervene to turn the talk back to

Women gossip at the market while goods are bought and sold.

subjects all Englishmen agreed upon: that their own failings brought on God's punishment, in the form of storms or smallpox; that all Englishmen must remain brothers in one united church; that King Charles had carried his royal authority too far and menaced the Englishman's hard-won right to an elected Parliament. In a parting toast, they congratulated themselves on belonging to a vital nation engaged in the race among European states to explore unknown continents and colonize distant lands.

Despite the delights of conversation, a yeoman took the road back out of town before dark. He wanted to reach home in time to lead his family and servants in their evening prayers and Bible reading, which would buttress them against the ways of the Devil. He might ask his sons to recite the Commandments or the Beatitudes, memorized at home or in school. His smartest sons went to the grammar school at eight years of age, where they mixed with the sons of merchants and clothiers, ministers and doctors, seamen and craftsmen. The boys learned Latin—writing themes, giving speeches, and speaking to each other in that tongue, still the language of scholarship. The brightest of these boys, if their parents could afford the expense, went on to the university at Oxford or Cambridge, where they prepared to be doctors and ministers, or to the Inns of Court in London to study law.

PERSECUTION AND COLONIZATION

The more that extreme Puritans talked about a church without bishops, the more King Charles and his bishops hated, even feared, all Puritans. In 1633, the king appointed William Laud to be Archbishop of Canterbury, the highest position in the Church of England. At this time, many of the parish ministers in England were poorly educated and idle, services were conducted in a variety of ways, Puritan ministers avoided the formal regulations, and parishioners behaved without respect in church. To overcome this slovenliness, which might drive people back toward Roman Catholicism, Laud tried to enforce uniform worship. He loved ritual and ceremony just as much as the Puritans detested it. He refused to consider a system of church government without bishops, and resolved to put an end to the Puritans by forbidding their lectures and censoring their writings.

He ordered every minister to don a white surplice, to bow at the mention of Jesus Christ, to follow word for word the service set down in the Prayer Book, and to cease giving and publishing sermons. Furthermore, he directed all ministers to read the following declaration every Sunday:

> . . . Our pleasure is, that after the end of divine service our good people be not disturbed, letted, or discouraged from any lawful recreation, such as dancing, either for men or women; archery for men, leaping, vaulting, or any other such lawful recreation, nor from having May-games, Whitsun-ales, and Morris-dancing; and the setting up of Maypoles and other sports therewith used.[3]

Some Puritan ministers refused to read this Declaration of Sports.

Challenging authority even in this small way took courage, since almost everyone in Norwich had heard of Puritans punished for speaking out. The most severe case came in 1637 when three Puritan extremists, Bastwick, Burton, and Prynne, whose writings attacked the bishops and the church courts, were called before the Star Chamber, a special court made up of the king's privy council and two judges, who simply carried out the king's will. Each of the accused men was made to stand with his head and hands locked in a pillory. After two hours, their ears were cut off, and Prynne was branded on both cheeks with the letters "S.L." for "Seditious Libeler." All three were sentenced to heavy fines and put into prison for life. It was thought that making a public spectacle of a condemned man would help to prevent the recurrence of his crime; but, instead, each punishment of a Puritan produced great sympathy for their cause.

In 1635, Bishop Corbet died and Laud had Matthew Wren appointed Bishop of Norwich. Wren hated the Puritans as much as Laud did and had the power to forbid them ever to preach again or conduct marriage or burial services anywhere in England. Under Bishop Wren, life grew difficult for the dozen or more Puritan ministers around the town. If Wren accused them of preaching Puritan ideas, they could be called before a Court of High Commission made up of Anglican clergymen. Puritans could expect little sympathy from this court which invariably found suspects guilty of ignoring Anglican ritual, disobeying the king, and trying to overthrow both church and state. If the suspect did not recant immediately, he was imprisoned, and he was fined so much money that his wife and children were left penniless. It is not surprising that a few Puritan ministers died in jail, for cells were cold and damp and food scarce.

To avoid fines and imprisonment, a minister called before the High Commission Court usually admitted his guilt. So doing, he was allowed to keep on preaching, provided he stuck to the Anglican ritual and paid the cost of the trial and a fine. Naturally, the Puritan ministers of Norwich did not want to be caught, and because they never knew when a representative sent by Bishop Wren or Archbishop Laud might be sitting in the congregation, they stopped preaching their beliefs. Nevertheless, Puritan ministers in Norwich probably did what their colleagues all over England did—held secret meetings on Sunday afternoons in woods or garrets. No amount of persecution could stop these ministers and their followers from clinging to the principles they felt were essential for serving God and getting to heaven.

After Laud came to Canterbury and Wren to Norwich, Puritans in the town began to realize that they had lost the battle to reform the Church of England from within. Yet they were determined to preserve what they believed was God's true church even if they had to leave England to do so. Some Puritans had given up and left a few years earlier for the New World. They had forsaken comfortable homes, old friends, and convenient shops for a wilderness around Boston Harbor in Massachusetts Bay Colony where they had to clear land, build houses, dig wells, get along without a town, and encounter Indians. They were, however, able to worship as they believed all Englishmen should, and to set up the sort of representative government that King Charles had denied them.

Puritans in Norwich waited eagerly for news from Massachusetts Bay Colony. Reports of food shortages and deaths from scurvy, and accounts of being cheated in trade by the Indians discouraged the hesitant. Descriptions of fertile land, plenty of fish, and abundant stone and timber encouraged the willing. In the market place, in shops, and in homes all around Norwich, Puritans perused pamphlets such as one written by John Winthrop, the governor of Massachusetts Bay Colony. He assured them that they could better serve God by building His Church in the wilderness and by spreading the gospel to the Indians than they could by struggling in vain to reform the church at home. He pointed out, too, that prices in England were high and towns crowded, whereas in New England men could have hundreds of acres of farmland, and craftsmen, who were few and far between, could find plenty of work.

These urgings appealed to Puritan ministers in Norwich who worried about a summons from Bishop Wren. Some left quickly to escape being called before the High Commission Court. Others had time to organize members of their parishes to leave with them, waiting for the sale of houses and leases, shops and cattle. Parish members boarded ships in family groups, hoping to rejoin other members of their parish on the New England shore.

During the 1630's, nearly twenty thousand men, women, and children, left England to settle the Massachusetts Bay Colony. They departed in largest numbers from trading towns like Norwich that were Puritan strongholds. Half the emigrants who left Norwich were Puritans. Many of them were workers dependent upon the faltering cloth industry, freedom-loving men unhappy about the king's dismissal of Parliament and the levy of ship money, yeomen who wanted to get away from poor harvests and to own land, younger sons of yeomen who wanted to continue farming, craftsmen without monopolies who could find no work, laborers who could not pay the increasingly high food prices brought about by the poor harvests, and seamen and apprentices bound for adventure. There were even a few saddened people looking for a new life who had lost their families during one of several epidemics of plague that had swept Norwich and other crowded towns during the 1630's.

Few Puritan country gentlemen or rich merchants left Norwich. They had too much money, position, and comfort to lose. Most doctors and lawyers remained where their practices were, even though many of them were Puritans. The poorest did not leave Norwich either, laborers with no money to buy tools or learn a craft could not raise the money for passage across the Atlantic. A few did manage to go by binding themselves as indentured servants and promising to work four to seven years in exchange for passage.

Some of the men who left Norwich took their wives, children, and servants with them. Others struck out alone for the wilderness to prepare the way for their families who would follow. Whatever their reasons for leaving, spinners, knitters, dyers, weavers, clothiers, and a few wool merchants abandoned their homes in town and started their journey. Goldsmiths, grocers, carpenters. blacksmiths, and teachers carried or carted their bundles over one of the river's five bridges and out to the high road that ran east to the sea. In the countryside, yeomen gathered up clothing, furniture, utensils, and a good supply of food from their cottages. They sold their leases, but took their horses and cows and chickens. These emigrants began their journey to the New World by walking or riding the twenty-four miles to Yarmouth, where they boarded a vessel bound across the ocean. Nearly two months later, these Englishmen sailed into the harbor at Boston, where they anchored their ship and rowed ashore to a settlement that flew an English flag at the edge of the unexplored American continent. Arriving in large numbers, these immigrants made Massachusetts Bay the most quickly settled colony England ever claimed in the race for the New World.

FROM FREEDOM

The African Gold Coast, 1731

THE FORTRESS AT CAPE COAST

During the 1700's, townsmen and villagers were taken as slaves from almost the entire west coast of Africa between Senegal in the north and Angola in the south. Each year from 1700 to 1750, about ten thousand men, women, and children from a small stretch of that area, the Gold Coast, were bound in chains, loaded onto boats, rowed out to slave ships anchored at sea, herded down into holds, and shipped to America. In the European colonies of North and South America and the West Indies, the slaves worked on large sugar, tobacco, and cotton plantations. The European colonists themselves were not accustomed to agricultural labor in hot climates. American Indians, forced to plant and harvest the land that had been their own, usually died on the job or escaped into the woods. Africans, it was found, could survive the hard work in the open fields and turn in a good profit for their owners.

Many slaves passed through the English trading fort

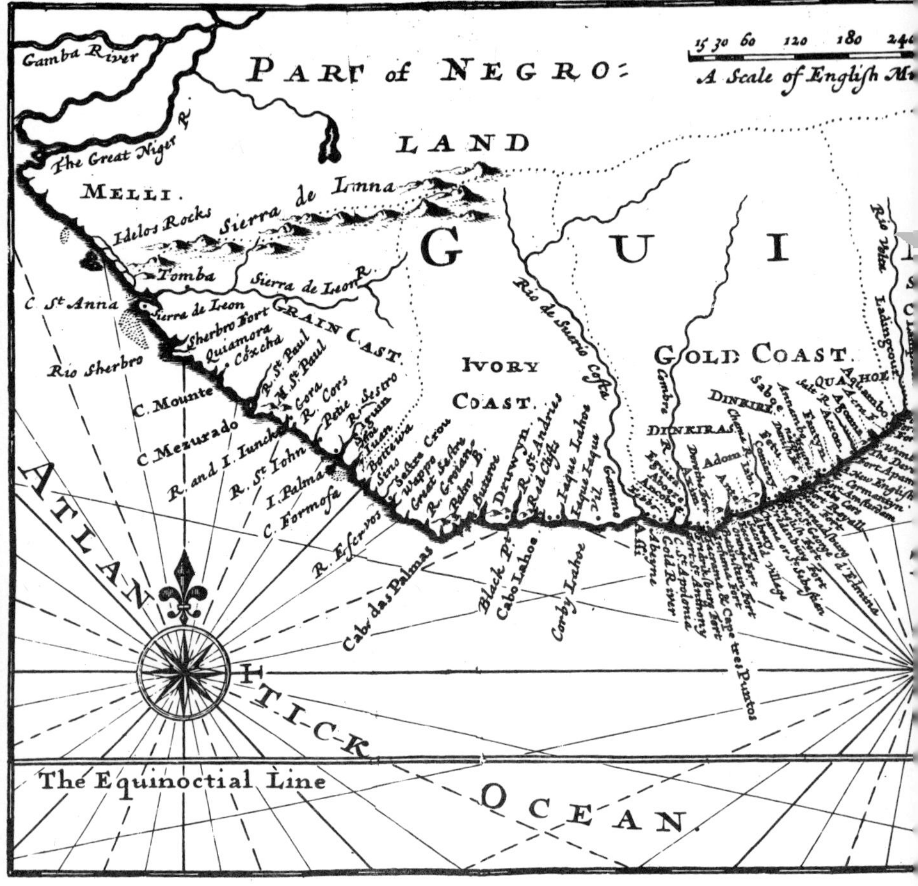

at Cape Coast on their way out of Africa. The Portuguese had settled at Cape Coast first, in 1610, and had built a castle on the headland. Thereafter, the castle was captured and enlarged in turn by the Swedes, the Danes, and the Dutch, with the English finally taking it from the Dutch in 1664. From the open end of the castle quadrangle, thirteen brass cannon pointed seaward to prevent

On this early map of coastal West Africa, the town of Cape Coast (called by its Portuguese name of Cabo Cors) is located near the midpoint of the Gold Coast's shoreline. The Fanti (Fantyn) tribe is situated in the same area. Three inland points mentioned in the text but not shown on this map are: Manso, 30 miles north-northwest of Cape Coast; Banso, 90 miles north; Kibi, 140 miles east-northeast.

any enemy ship from anchoring in the harbor. Forty more heavy cannon, mounted on high, thick walls, formed the defenses on the other three sides. Within the castle walls lived over a hundred Englishmen—a governor, a commercial agent, a minister, a physician, various financial administrators, workmen, and soldiers—and a hundred African soldiers and laborers. There was a dun-

The women of Cape Coast do laundry and prepare for market.

geon room big enough to hold a thousand slaves. Strong defenses were needed both to control the imprisoned Africans and to hold the fort against the rival Dutch, a short distance to the west at Elmina Castle, with whom they had many skirmishes.

Seeking the protection of the English fort and a chance to trade, African farmers, fisherman, craftsmen, and merchants from several coastal tribes had come to live near Cape Coast Castle. The women of the town held a market every day while the men went fishing in their canoes. Most townsmen lived in mud houses along crooked narrow streets. A few two-story buildings belonged to local merchants who had grown rich trading with the English. A chief of the Fanti tribe claimed the land on which Cape Coast Castle stood, and the English paid him rent for it. He forebade the English ever to travel inland to the villages on the coastal plain or to the rain forest beyond to bargain for slaves, and insisted that this business be handled by the African merchants on the coast.

Although the first Europeans to come to Cape Coast asked for gold, it was not long before they began to want slaves. At first, merchants of the Fanti tribe, the most powerful tribe on the coast, sold to the Europeans their own domestic slaves. These were men, women, and children who had fallen into slavery through defeat in war, through debt or crime, or who were the offspring of slaves. Since time immemorial, the strong have enslaved the weak in Africa and in many parts of the world. As the demand increased, the Fanti merchants enslaved more of their tribesmen to sell. When these ran out, the Fanti began to kidnap strangers and to send men inland to raid neighboring tribes or to trade for captives. In the 1730's, Fanti slavers from Cape Coast were carrying English guns and cloth about thirty miles inland to exchange for slaves captured by merchants of the Ashanti tribe.

The Ashanti Union had been formed during the 1600's when a number of smaller states, all descended from a

Cape Coast Castle, standing securely on the coast, had attracted Africans to settle in a town nearby. From Cape Coast, Fanti slavers traveled inland to meet Ashanti merchants with captives to sell.

people known as the Akan, got together to form a confederation against attacking tribes. As these states together conquered their enemies, the Union grew, becoming the strongest nation in the forest north of Cape Coast. Enemy captives were sold as slaves, and the guns received in exchange enabled the Ashanti to capture more enemies to trade for more European muskets and cloth. As the demand for slaves continued to grow, a state of perpetual warfare developed among the tribes on the plain and in the rain forest, each trying to take captives

they could exchange for European guns with which to protect themselves from the Ashanti.

Many of the Ashanti's victims came from the independent state of Akim. These people, too, were descendants of the Akan. Ashanti armies had first conquered Akim in 1702, but for almost thirty years the people had refused to pay tribute. In 1731, the Ashanti armies again invaded Akim, attacking towns and villages. One of these villages might have been Banso, located in a hilly district near the western edge of Akim.

BANSO, A VILLAGE IN THE RAIN FOREST

Banso lay in a clearing in the tropical rain forest roughly ninety miles inland from Cape Coast. Written records concerning Banso do not exist, but if it looked like other African villages, Banso's two unpaved streets ran the length and breadth of the village and met at its center. At this intersection, villagers gathered to buy and sell, hear the news of the day, and hold celebrations. Narrow lanes branched off these streets and wound among clusters of huts. Nearly a hundred circular huts with sun-baked mud walls and cone-shaped thatched roofs stood close together within the village.

The single low doorway of each hut faced southwest to receive the prevailing wind. On the dirt floor of the hut, the hearth was surrounded by a circular mound of earth that symbolized the moon's orbital path and round face. The Akim revered that heavenly body because they believed that the founder of their state had been the Daughter of the Moon. On the ground enclosed by the hut there were rush mats for sleeping, one or two low wooden stools, probably a table, a few earthenware pots, a water jar, several wooden bowls, and some large open gourds called calabashes. The only other possessions that the average villager had were domestic animals—perhaps a dog, a few goats and chickens, possibly a sheep or two, and several pigs.

The Akim people of Banso kept their Akan beliefs and customs. Each person belonged to one of the seven clans of the Akim tribe, and believed he was descended from an ancestress who had herself descended from an animal. Children of each clan were taught never to kill or eat their own clan animal whether it was a frog, bat, crow, mole, buffalo, parrot, or hawk. All Akan people believed that two basic ingredients made up every human being—"blood" inherited from his mother and "spirit" derived from his father. Although a boy learned from his father how to plant crops and trap animals, how to weave cloth or carve wood, he belonged to his mother's clan; he traced his descent through her, and lived with her while he was young. Often a woman's children went to live with her brother when they reached adolescence, since it was from him, not their own father, that they would inherit land.

A man could have several wives, but he had to choose them from a clan other than his own. The richer he was, the more wives he had, but few Banso villagers had more than one or two. When a man had more than one wife, each woman usually lived in a separate hut. A man's hut stood near those of his mother's brothers and of his own married brothers. The men of each family group and their wives took pride in keeping their section of the village neat. The women swept the lanes between the huts, and the men weeded them and made gutters.

Each family group had a leader, and all the leaders formed a council of elders to manage the affairs of Banso and to select, from among themselves, the village headman. He and the rest of the elders held their meetings upon a stage of woven cane built near the headman's hut. The headman would listen to discussions, which often became heated, and would make occasional remarks. When he felt all views had been aired, he summarized the discussion, but the council as a whole settled disputes between villagers, punished a murderer, or decided to repulse an attack by an enemy tribe.

On most religious occasions, the family leader made a sacrifice to the dead members of his family. He carried a bowl of mashed plantain (large coarse bananas) or yams (like sweet potatoes) mixed with egg and palm wine to a separate hut where special carved stools were kept. Each stool had belonged to an elder, and when he had died it had been smeared with a mixture of soot and egg yolk. Placing a spoonful of the mashed plaintain or yam on each of the heirloom stools, the family leader prayed for the welfare of his family in words similar to those the headman used when he made sacrifices on behalf of the entire village:

> My spirit grandfathers . . . come and receive this mashed plantain and eat; let this town prosper; and permit the bearers of children to bear children; and may all the people who are in this town get riches.[1]

Then he scattered the remainder of the plantain or yam on the ground outside the hut, and the rest of the family joined him in drinking palm wine.

Because the Akan people believed that their dead existed in a spirit world and could plead with the creator Sky God on behalf of the living, it was important to offer sacrifices and keep on good terms with one's ancestors. If a farmer cut himself while felling a tree, if drought ruined his crops, or if disease killed his son, he often considered the disaster a punishment, brought about by his ancestors, for his own misdeeds. An Akan regarded an insult to his ancestors as more offensive than a blow to himself—"Strike me but do not curse my mother," [2] he would say.

Fields surrounded the village, and when the soil became exhausted, the farmers abandoned it and cleared new land from the forest. They cut down trees and brush with heavy iron knives and burned away what remained. Although the land actually belonged to the dead ancestors, the family leaders gave the head of each household the right to use a piece of it. Men, women, and children worked together in the fields, planting, weeding, and harvesting yams, grain, and plantains to feed their families. Farmers stored their harvested crops in sun-baked mud bins nearly ten feet high. These bins stood near the fields on rings of large stones to raise them clear of white ants and other pests. Removable grass roofs protected the contents from the harmattan, a strong, dust-laden wind from the Sahara. To please the spirit of Earth, there was no work on the land every seventh day, the birthday of Earth. At seed time, a farmer stood on the land and said such words as these:

> Grandfather So-and-so, you (once) came and hoed here and then you left (it) to me. You also Earth, Ya, on whose soil I am going to hoe, the yearly cycle has come round and I am going to cultivate; when I work let a fruitful year come upon me, do not let the knife cut me, do not let a tree break and fall upon me, do not let a snake bite me.[3]

Whether laboring in the fields or at some other job, the slaves and freemen of Banso worked side by side. There may have been more slaves than freemen, but the distinction between the two was almost unrecognizable. A slave could marry, live with his family, and own property, including other slaves. A slave woman could marry a freeman and, if she did, her children would be free. A master often rewarded a hard-working slave by granting him freedom. Trusted slaves took long trips to do business for their masters. Others were honored craftsmen with many privileges. Most slaves, however, worked the land, keeping some of the crops and giving the rest to their masters.

The people of Banso ate just about the same food every day. They began the day at sunrise with gruel made of pounded grain and water, flavored with some common fruit such as tamarind or pineapple. In the early afternoon, they lunched on pudding with a butter made from seeds. Shortly afterward, the women and girls left the fields, collected food and firewood and began to prepare the biggest meal of the day. They pounded yam or grain into paste and boiled it. Peppers or other vegetables, herbs, or bits of meat or fish that had been cooked to a sauce in palm oil, were added to the pot. The children carried a portion of this meal to the house where all the men in the family ate together. Everyone offered his first morsel of food and drops of palm wine or beer brewed from grain to his ancestors, and each left a bit of food for them in his dish at the end of the meal.

Though the diet was not varied, it was nourishing enough and could make the people physically tough and able to work hard. Yet the insect-carried diseases of West Africa—malaria, yellow fever, sleeping sickness, and dengue fever—sapped some of their strength and brought numerous deaths. Parasites in their blood or bodies made even children feel tired much of the time. Bad drinking water and dust on food caused dysentery, and the shortage of water for washing encouraged skin disease. When they were sick, the people of Banso used herbs or made sacrifices to speed recovery. No matter how much sorrow parents felt when a child died, they dared not mourn very much, for fear that showing grief would attract Death, who loved watching people in pain, and encourage him to take away even more children.

During the dry season when there was little work in the fields, men hunted deer and wild fowl with bows and arrows. Often they went fishing. Lying on their stomachs on wide planks, they would paddle out into a lake and drop their nets. When these were filled, they dove under the water and carried the nets up. At other times, they might look for gold. Every man in Banso was permitted to dig for gold in the hills and every woman to pan it in the streams near the village. Akim had grown wealthy from exporting gold mined by slaves, and gold dust was used as money. People who found gold were permitted to keep a third of it, but they had to give the rest to the village headman.

The dry season gave the people of Banso time to make cloth. The poorest slaves wore cloth made of the bark which they stripped from the *kyenkyen* tree in long pieces about a foot wide. They laid the strips, softened in water, over a fallen tree trunk and beat them with wooden mallets until they were almost three times as wide. Most people, however, wore cotton cloth. The women grew the cotton, spun it into thread, and dyed it. Then men, who had learned to weave on toy looms when they were boys, wove the thread into brilliant color schemes in a tremendous variety of patterns. Women cut and sewed the woven cloth into loose fitting robes for themselves and their families. The women wore brass rings on their arms and ankles, and ivory or copper rings or beautiful shells in their hair. So dressed, they carried calabashes on their heads filled with grain, yams, peppers, plantains, palm kernels, and spun cotton to the market where the two main streets of Banso crossed. Other women who made clay pots carried these in huge nets on their heads. The women traded these products with the village craftsmen for wooden bowls and stools, woven baskets, arm rings, iron tools, and arrow points.

The few rich men in Banso had probably acquired their wealth through engaging in the slave trade or by carrying gold and kola nuts (caffeine-containing seeds chewed as a stimulant) through the forest to its northern edge, where the trans-Sahara route discharged copper and blankets. Few of Banso's craftsmen and farmers ever ventured beyond their own fields, but they knew of distant territories and chiefs. Banso and other villages for miles around made up the Division of Western Akim. The headmen of all these villages formed a council and selected a chief. Each headman promised the chief that his village would defend the land in time of war. He promised to send men to work on the chief's farm several days each year and to pay him yearly tributes of yams, grain, and palm oil. He sent the chief a share of any gold found in his village or of any large animal killed there. The chief of the Western Division sat in the great council of the whole independent nation of Akim. This council met at Kibi, the capital of Akim, and governed the nation under the leadership of a single supreme chief, the *omanhene*. All the people of Akim felt loyalty to the omanhene and strove to preserve their freedom against invading Ashanti armies. They were not always successful.

RAID AT BANSO AND MARCH TO THE COAST

The villagers often gathered during the evenings in the headman's compound, especially during the dry season when there was little work in the fields to tire them. The village musicians brought their drums, gourd rattles, iron gongs, stringed instruments, long wooden flutes, and horns made from elephants' tusks. On moonlit nights the singing and dancing and drumming continued until well after midnight.

Let us imagine that one evening a war cry and a volley of musket shots interrupted the night's music and dancing. Having set fire to the thatched huts, about thirty raiders rushed in from all sides with leveled muskets. The unarmed villagers at first ran in confusion and then huddled together in fear. The attackers were Ashanti merchants who traded peacefully by day and raided by night. They had lain in wait in the forest until nightfall and then had moved in on the huts of Banso.

As some of the Ashanti pointed guns, others seized the strongest and tallest young men and women and some of the older children and bound their wrists together with bamboo withes. Then they clamped iron shackles on their ankles—the right ankle of one man to the left ankle of another. Anyone who tried to resist was immediately shot as a warning to the others. To the crack of a lash and the shout of commands, close to a hundred of the healthiest villagers stumbled slowly into the unknown beyond their homes, leaving behind the oldest men, some of the women, and the small children, wailing and defenseless.

For over a week, the Banso captives marched along a trade route cut through the dense forest, always with the fear of a musket shot or a lash from behind. Undoubtedly, some of them noted each twist of the path in hopes that they could find their way back to Banso if they were ever able to escape. They walked about eight hours a day, making brief stops to rest, drink, or eat as it pleased their captors. Some nights were spent huddled in the market places of prosperous towns, others in the burned-out remains of raided villages. From time to time, they would pass caravans of traders with their loads on their heads, marching in single file along the narrow jungle paths.

The caravan of slaves moved slowly. Huge trunks of fallen trees and roots of cottonwoods cluttered the paths that wound through the dense undergrowth. The only relief from the heat of the tropical sun came from the shadows cast by the masses of leaves at the tops of the trees, some a hundred feet tall, and the twisting network of vines that hung from the upper branches and trailed brilliant flowers. The chains that bound the captives made each step exhausting and painful. Those who could not keep up were whipped and dragged along. Many died on the march and were simply unchained and left at the

An exchange of captives for guns, liquor, and cloth.

side of the path. Occasionally the caravan crossed rivers swarming with crocodiles or passed through clearings where the captives saw village huts and free tribesmen watching flocks of goats. Finally the route emerged from the rain forest onto the more open coastal plain.

The caravan stopped at Manso, a town on the edge of the forest where African traders from the forest met African traders from the coast. Manso's houses were larger than the huts of Banso, rectangular in shape, and carefully laid out along streets. The market area was larger also and busier than anything the Banso villagers had ever seen, and the traders who circulated throughout the market place spoke a variety of languages. In all directions, the Banso captives saw traders seated on the ground with their wares spread out in front of them, some under awnings and some in the open. The range of goods for sale seemed endless: beef and mutton cut in small pieces for soup; wild hog, deer, and monkey flesh; chickens and skins; yams, corn, and rice; peppers, oranges, pineapples, and plantains; salt and dried fish from the coast; palm wine and rum; pipes, beads, calabashes, mirrors, and sandals; cotton cloth and colored thread.

The Ashanti seemed to have their own special location in the market and here they lined up their captives. Shortly, some Fanti slavers from Cape Coast came to offer guns, gunpowder, liquor, and cloth in exchange for the caravan of slaves from Banso. Bargaining took little time, since past experience had roughly determined how much a slave or a gun was worth in terms of gold dust. When they reached an agreement, the Ashanti raiders picked up the European goods and headed back to the forest, leaving the Banso captives in the hands of the middlemen from Cape Coast.

After another week of traversing rocky countryside, the exhausted captives were finally led into Cape Coast and then into outdoor pens made of wooden poles, reinforced with iron bars, and roofed with thatch. Some of the slavers stood guard over them with loaded muskets. Other slavers reported the arrival of the captives to the Fanti broker, describing the sturdy quality of the villagers they had brought to the coast. The slavers probably received no pay, since in most cases they were slaves themselves. Their only reward would be the broker's approval for a healthy, salable batch of men and women.

INTO ENGLISH HANDS

The Fanti broker might have gone immediately to the castle to talk price with the English factor, or commercial agent. Once the broker and the factor agreed on the price, the slavers brought their Akim captives, naked, close-shaven, and glossy with palm oil, into the castle quadrangle. The oil made it hard for the English to tell the young captives from the old. The English physician at the castle examined the slaves, feeling the muscles of their arms and legs, looking carefully at their teeth, making them jump several times and stretch out their arms rapidly to test their wind and limbs. He looked for evidence of smallpox, which would spread rapidly in the crowded conditions of a slave ship. Anyone who looked older than thirty-five or had a maimed arm or leg, missing teeth, gray hair, or film over his eyes was rejected. Later these abandoned captives would be freed, but they would probably die before they found their way back to Banso.

When the English factor had agreed with the physician's selection, he and and Fanti broker signed the necessary papers and the captives, usually about two-thirds of them men, passed to the hands of the factor. In exchange, the broker received, in quantity equal to the agreed value of the slaves, whatever European goods he wanted from the castle warehouse—guns and gunpowder, tobacco, molasses, liquor, colored cloth, cutlasses and knives, pewter dishes, copper pots, or beads. After reserving a portion for the local Fanti chief and selecting some things for himself, the broker would turn the rest over to his slavers for their next trip inland to buy slaves.

Exactly how much slaves cost is very hard to say today,

since they were bartered for goods and the value of slaves and goods in terms of gold dust changed constantly. We do know that a European factor paid about twice as much for a slave in 1750 as he had in 1708 and that a slave woman cost somewhat less than a man. In one transaction "a man and a fine girl" were bartered for:

> One roll of tobacco, one string pipe coral
> One gun, three cutlasses, one brass blunderbuss
> Twenty-four linen handkerchiefs, 5 patches, 3 jugs rum
> Twelve Britannicas, 12 pint mugs
> One laced hat, one linen handkerchief.[4]

The fact that a man or woman could be sold for goods reflected the new status the Africans would have as slaves in America. Men who had been free or, at worst, slaves with certain freedoms and privileges, would not be treated as human beings but as property in the New World.

When the exchange was completed, the captives, still in chains, were branded on the right breast or shoulder with DY (Duke of York), the mark of the English trading company which now owned them. They were then locked in dungeons below the castle quadrangle, where they waited for the next slave ship to arrive.

As soon as a ship anchored off Cape Coast, all available African slavers came to the castle to help load the slaves. The march to the beach brought the captives closer to the sea than they had ever been before, and the

Slavers paddle to ships off Manfro, east of Cape Coast.

roar of the surf and the breaking waves of the Atlantic terrified them. Some of the slaves, resisting the lash,

> . . . flung themselves on the beach, clutching handfuls of sand in a desperate effort to remain in Africa. Some tried to strangle themselves with their chains; but the slavers . . . were prepared for every form of rebellion. . . . The slaves were beaten, pushed, dragged, and even carried to the big canoes . . . which were waiting to ferry them through the surf.[5]

Being loaded into canoes only intensified the will of the captives to remain in Africa. As the captain of one European slaving vessel wrote:

> The negroes are so wilful and loth to leave their own country, that they have often leap'd out of the canoos, boat and ship, into the sea, and kept under water till they were drowned, to avoid being taken up and saved by our boats which pursued them.[6]

Africans who drowned themselves within sight of their native shores, or starved themselves to death on shipboard, hoped to rejoin their ancestors in a life after death.

Those who lived to reach American shores were usually unloaded at Barbados, Jamaica, Antigua, or some other English island in the West Indies and sold to plantation owners there who would "season" them. Seasoning meant accustoming the Africans to their captive existence and familiarizing them with the English language, and with different food, clothing, and farming methods, in addition to working them extremely hard. A few years later, some of these Africans were transported to Charleston, Norfolk, Newport, and other ports in the English colonies in North America. Being subjected to one ordeal after another before reaching America and being separated from fellow tribesmen after arriving here, the Africans were seldom able to share memories of freedom or continue time-honored traditions from their African past.

FROM FAMINE

Skibbereen, Ireland, 1845-1848

SURROUNDED BY POTATO FIELDS

The one long main street that curved through Skibbereen ran from substantial buildings at one end of town to squalor at the other. Large stone buildings, a courthouse and jail, an infantry barrack, several churches and chapels, a school, and a dispensary stood at the eastern end. Toward the center of town was a market square, busy enough on weekdays, but especially so on Saturdays. Here lived the tradespeople of Skibbereen—the shopkeeper who sold seeds, salt, and oatmeal, the carpenter who built chests and tables, the tailor who made warm woolen coats, the wandering trader who collected eggs from the farms, and the dealer who bought grain from farmers and shipped it to England. The houses of most of the five thousand inhabitants were crowded together at the western end. Some of these people worked in the brewery or the flour mill on the outskirts of town, but many had no jobs at all. Poor laborers, beggars, homeless persons, penniless widows, and starving children lived in rat-infested cabins; they had no water supply or sewage system, no street lighting or police protection. Piles of filth were never cleared away from the streets and muddy lanes.

Many would have called the town ugly, but it stood among beautiful rolling hills kept green by almost continual rains. Shrubs and rocks dotted the hillsides but there were no trees. The river Ilen flowed into a pic-

turesque bay beyond which stretched the Atlantic Ocean. Vast dreary boglands covered the valleys between the green hills.

In the country district around Skibbereen, peasants lived in small cottages beside the roads and grew potatoes in the boggy soil nearby. The only tool a peasant owned was a spade. The only crop he could raise enough of on his small plot to feed his large family was the potato.

A view of Old Chapel Lane, a street in Skibbereen, during the famine years.

A family of five or six could live for a year on the potatoes that an acre and a half of land provided. Grain for the same family would have taken three to five times as much land, more elaborate tools, and a greater knowledge of tillage.

A ten-mile trip to another village seemed a long journey to the people of Skibbereen. They knew little about Ireland or its inhabitants. But if they imagined that country people elsewhere in Ireland led a life as simple as their own, they were right.

A young woman takes carefully packed eggs to market.

As throughout Ireland, the people of Skibbereen were very religious. Men, women, and children went to mass at the Roman Catholic chapel every Sunday, and many attended on weekdays as well. At noon and at six in the evening, when the church bells rang the Angelus, they knelt down and said their prayers, whether they were in the field or at home. They never began a meal without first saying grace. If they passed people at work in a field, they said, "God bless your work," and the reply was always, "God save you too."[1]

The peasants owned no land. They were tenants, cultivating soil that belonged to someone else. Ireland had been invaded several times by the English, beginning in 1169, and now most of the land belonged to English landlords. Many of these landlords lived in England, and the stately mansions outside Skibbereen were seldom occupied. Their agents divided the land among the tenants and collected the rents.

The few really comfortable farmers in Skibbereen rented as many as thirty acres. The poorest held less than one. An average farm consisted of about three-and-a-half acres. On one of his acres, the farmer cultivated wheat and oats which he sold to pay his rent; on a second acre-and-a-half, he grazed his cow and grew and cut hay to feed it; on the remaining acre, he planted potatoes to feed his family. He raised a few "green crops"—cabbages, beans, kale—and some carrots and turnips in a separate small garden. A farmer had two or three pigs and possibly a few sheep, and his wife kept chickens. If he earned any extra money by weaving or by selling eggs, milk, butter, or a pig, he might rent another potato patch or simply hide the coins in the thatch of his cabin.

A farmer would promise an agent almost any rent to avoid losing his land. The crafty agent, knowing how desperate the farmer was for land, every year rented each plot to the highest bidder. As a result, the farmer paid an extraordinarily high rent for land that was often boggy, hilly, or rocky. If he could not pay, the agent evicted him and rented the land to someone who could or divided the landlord's estate into smaller holdings, spreading thirty farmers over the acres that had once supported twenty-five.

Understandably, the farmer hated the agent. Even more, he despised the landlord whom he had probably never seen. The landlord represented the Protestant English who had defeated the Irish, taken away Irish lands, and attempted to stamp out the Catholic religion. The absentee landlords of Skibbereen would not build cottages for their Irish tenants, pay for fences and gates, or manure and drain the fields. It was discouraging for a farmer to make any of these improvements himself, since he might be evicted at any moment.

Every year more and more poor farmers fell so far into debt that they were evicted. They became cottiers, too poor to rent even a tiny plot. Unless a cottier could find a scrap of soil on which to grow potatoes, his family would starve. He hired the use of an acre or less of ground from some farmer for a season. The farmer ploughed and manured the field. The cottier provided the seed and harvested the crop. He did all his work with a spade and, aside from a few green crops, he grew only potatoes.

The cottier paid the rent on his potato patch by working eighty to two hundred fifty days of the year for the farmer, mending fences, digging ditches, or planting and harvesting. A cottier had to buy his seeds, clothes for his family, and something else to eat when the potatoes ran out. He had to buy on credit at high interest from shopkeepers in Skibbereen, hoping to repay his debts after the harvest by selling some potatoes. Because he seldom handled money, the cottier did not know what it meant to save. When the potato crop yielded poorly, as it did from time to time, his family starved and their debts remained unpaid. The cottier had no regular job because Skibbereen had neither mines nor industry. Its brewery and flour mill employed only townsmen. The poor cottier might earn a few shillings by doing extra work for another farmer and, when desperate, by selling his pig.

The pig was the treasure of the Irish cottier and was treated accordingly. He slept in the hut with the family. He rooted out food in the neighboring bog and was fed potato peelings and boiled potatoes almost as good as those the cottier family ate themselves. Normally a cottier fattened his pig for two years before selling it to get the few shillings of cash with which he bought clothes, seed, and another pig.

In recent years the population of Ireland had increased, owing to an abundance of potatoes and the practice of marrying young and raising large families. Few of the children that Irish parents so fondly raised would go to school or grow up able to write their names, since they would work in the fields from an early age. Marrying and raising the next generation of children depended partly upon a young couple's finding land to farm. Many a farmer allowed his married son or daughter to occupy a section of his own land because the couple had nowhere else to go. As sons did the same for their children, farms decreased in size and more sons became simple cottiers. Eventually, as sons rented fractions of acres on their father's land, more and more of the land was devoted to potatoes and less to grain and green crops.

Cottiers and small farmers, who were both called peasants, lived in windowless mud cabins which they built themselves in three or four days whenever they leased a piece of land. First, they dug a shallow pit and then piled up walls of mud they had mixed with straw. Since heavy rains could wash away mud walls, they sometimes used loose stones instead, with green sods stuffed into the cracks between. The walls, about two feet thick, were rarely higher than seven feet. A roof of potato stalks, straw, or sods completed the humble dwelling. Father, mother, five or six children, and sometimes a grandfather or grandmother lived, ate, and slept together in the one-room cabin.

Holes in the thatch let in cold and rain as well as air and light. But peat that the peasants cut in summer from the surface of nearby bogs created a warm fire, no matter how damp the weather or how piercing the wind. Inside would be little more than an iron pot and a single stool. The family usually sat on stones. They rarely had a bed or blankets. Instead they slept on the damp floor or per-

Farmers lived in this high-ceilinged, windowed cottage.

haps on a pile of straw, sometimes covering themselves with layers of peat skimmed from the top of the bogs. Since the only outlets were the doorway and the holes in the roof, the cabins were smoky inside.

The more substantial farmers lived better than the peasants. The most well-off had cottages with whitewashed plaster walls, wooden rafters, a thatched roof, a door, and windows; they even constructed a chimney. The rest had two rooms instead of the cottier's one, a good roof, and a few tiny windows. There might be a pig sty or a separate shed for the cow, but seldom a proper barn. In their two rooms were found a number of stools, perhaps a wooden bench and table, a bedstead or two, with scanty bedding, some crockery, and a spinning wheel.

Despite their poverty, the peasants of Skibbereen were gay and lighthearted. Their potatoes required so little attention besides planting in spring and harvesting in summer and autumn that there was plenty of time left for simply enjoying the company of others. They spent their days and long winter nights in front of the peat fires in neighbors' cabins. They talked and laughed, told stories and jokes, and drank poteen, a strong whiskey distilled from potatoes or barley. In summer, neighbors frequently met at road intersections to dance to the music of a fiddle. They ignored everything else whenever there was a fair or a horse race, a wedding, or a funeral.

On these occasions men dressed up in red or black wool coats that were heavy enough to keep out the rain, blue corduroy trousers, bright vests, and felt hats. Colorful ribbons bedecked the women's caps, and their wool gowns were coquettishly arranged to reveal red or black flannel petticoats beneath.

Not every peasant family, however, could afford such dress outfits.

> In many poor hovels there is often only one complete suit between two individuals. . . [On Sunday] when one of the family has heard an early mass, he returns home, strips off his clothes, and gives them to the other, who goes to hear the second mass.[2]

For everyday use, peasants and farmers wore their

clothes until they became rags, and they seldom had shoes or stockings.

The peasants of Skibbereen ate almost nothing besides potatoes, for one, two, or three meals a day depending on how many potatoes they had. The more fortunate cottiers spent an occasional penny for a salt herring or several pennies for a half pound of bacon. A few did enjoy meat at Christmas time, but the majority never tasted it. Most peasants washed their meal down with water, though sometimes with poteen or tea.

Potatoes were simple to cook, and the peasant housewife knew how to prepare little else. She simply boiled them in a pot over the fire or threw them into the hot ashes and turned them. She drained the boiled potatoes in a basket, peeled them with her long thumbnail, and salted them.

Most families ate with their fingers, taking each potato from the basket and dipping it into a saucer of water or, if they could afford it, milk. At least potatoes made a nourishing diet, and children reared on them grew to healthy adults.

The literature of the time reflected the peasants' contentment with their simple life.

> . . . On winter nights, when the storm is sweeping over the hills, and the rain pattering furiously against the door, how happy, how truly felicitious to sit in a circle all round the fire, to hear the pot boiling, to see the beautiful roots bursting their coats, and showing their fair faces, to hold the herring on the point of a fork till it fizzes into an eating

> condition, to see the milk poured out into all the jugs, and to see the happy faces, and listen to the loud laughter of the children—Oh! give me a winter night, a turf fire, a rasher of bacon, and a mealy potatoe! [3]

As long as there were enough potatoes in the pot, the people seemed happy.

But there were not always enough. Disease or the wrong combination of sun and rain could damage the potatoes as they grew and so bring disaster to Skibbereen. Early every spring, families planted the eyes cut from last season's potatoes. Throughout the summer, they anxiously watched their fields, worrying about the lightning, and the threatening wind that withered the stalks, the drought that parched the ground, or the rain that flooded the planted rows.

The summer months brought suspense as the peasants watched the last season's supply of potatoes dwindle and the new stalks grow. A potato crop could be kept no longer than a few months, so that a surplus from a good season could not be stored against famine in the next. It was during the "meal months" of June, July, and August that the old potatoes either decayed or ran out, and many peasants had to eat oatmeal. They bought it on credit from a grain dealer in Skibbereen and had to repay almost twice the original price after the harvest.

No one could be certain how good the crop would be until the digging began. The main harvest was dug in September and October, with some potatoes dug earlier, and some dug as late as December and January. A full crop asured the peasants of food for another year, and turned their suspense into rejoicing.

FAMINE

At the beginning of July 1845, the weather was hot and dry and all seemed well with the potato crop. Then a sudden change brought three weeks of cold and rain. In October, the worried peasants of Skibbereen were relieved that the potatoes they dug up and put into storage pits in the fields looked healthy. Yet when they opened these pits a few weeks later, they found slimy, decaying masses of rotten potatoes. Blight (a moisture-loving fungus unidentified at the time) had ruined about half the crop. Terror gripped the people, for their potatoes would be gone by early spring.

Throughout the winter, they survived on whatever healthy and partially diseased potatoes they had, and other scraps of food. By spring, the poorest peasants began to starve, and fever from eating rotten potatoes became widespread. As people starved, they watched something unbearable. Good grain, livestock, and dairy products were shipped from Skibbereen to England. This produce would have fed the people, but they had no money to buy it. The farmers who supplied these things had to sell them abroad in order to get money to pay their rents.

The cheapest food available in Skibbereen was Indian corn, which the British government had quickly imported from America after the bad harvest. The government set some of the people of Skibbereen to work building and repairing roads so they could earn money to buy the corn. But the eightpence for a day's work did not go far to feed a family on corn meal that itself cost two pence a pound. One day eight hundred men, hired near Skibbereen to break stones for macadamizing the roads, struck and marched into town, their spades over their shoulders. They claimed they were unable to support their families on the wages they were receiving. Officials in town feared a riot, but the justice of the peace managed to stave it off by distributing biscuits and wages.

That spring, farmers and cottiers planted fewer potatoes than usual—some because they had eaten the potatoes they would normally have used for seed. Others planted less because they had abandoned their fields in order to earn wages on the public works projects. Despite the small planting, the people of Skibbereen were optimistic; they believed a good harvest always followed a bad one. Often in the past, they had survived a year of shortage, but no one remembered two such years in a row.

In late July, the potato plants bloomed and seemed healthy, but a week later the leaves had all turned black. Beneath the ground the peasants found potatoes the size of eggs, their skins covered with black patches. The stench was almost unbearable. Helpless peasants could be seen "seated on the fences of their decaying gardens, wringing their hands and wailing bitterly [at] the destruction that had left them foodless." [4]

The last season's blight had ruined only some of the potatoes, but in the autumn of 1846 the entire crop was lost, not only in Skibbereen but throughout Ireland. There were no potatoes at all, and the harvest of grain and vegetables was poor. One day in September, absolutely no bread or meal could be found in the market at Skibbereen. The following week the British government distributed two-and-a-half tons of meal, and it disappeared immediately. Some starving families walked miles into Skibbereen to get a little meal but arrived to find it all gone.

The people lived on blackberries and old cabbage leaves, roots and rotten turnips; they searched the fields time and time again looking for any edible remnants. By the end of October, the emaciated people were living on nettles and roadside weeds, but as autumn passed into winter, even these disappeared, and they turned to the beaches for seaweed and limpets. Without food, happiness vanished. There were no more marriage festivals or other forms of merriment. Hungry children, "their limbs wasted almost to the bone [sat] in groups by the cabin doors, making no attempt to play." [5]

Mothers who could not feed all their children begged officials to take two or three of them into the workhouse where they would be given food twice a day. In return, the children would break stones, spin, knit, and do other odd jobs. Many children were near death upon arrival at the workhouse and more than half died there.

Outside the workhouse, deaths from starvation occurred daily. Half-frozen corpses lay unburied in the streets, lanes, and cabins of Skibbereen. A visitor described the scene in one hovel that he entered:

> . . . Six famished and ghastly skeletons, to all appearances dead, were huddled in a corner on some

Men, women, and children try to gain entry to a workhouse.

> filthy straw, their sole covering what seemed a ragged horsecloth, their wretched legs hanging about, naked above the knees. I approached with horror, and found by a low moaning they were alive—they were in fever, four children, a woman and what had once been a man. [6]

A harsh winter added to the suffering. Normally, Skibbereen saw little frost or snow. But at the end of October 1846, it turned cold, and in November snow startled the people. Frost, snow, and grating winds continued into spring. April brought more piercing gales and hail.

And then, as if starvation and a harsh winter were not enough, the diseases, such as typhus, that accompany famine began to ravage the land. Poor sanitation and over-crowding in Skibbereen invited the spread of these diseases. Outside the town itself there was less crowding but sanitation was no better. Trickling manure heaps choked the doorways of the roadside cabins. Many of the poorest people were infested with lice. By now the peasants were filthy. They had pawned every stitch of clothing and bedding they could spare to buy food. Most did not have the strength to carry water for washing themselves and their few remaining rags of clothing. During January and February of 1847, people stood crowded together on the public works or huddled close enough for warmth but too close for health around the fires in their cabins. Diseased beggars drifted aimlessly from town to town. By March 1847, scarcely a house in Skibbereen was without fever.

People died of fever in the streets and were buried without coffins in common graves. In fear of fever, parents abandoned their children, and children deserted their parents. Neighbors, who had always been kindhearted, would no longer enter a cabin to help sick friends. Fever victims died alone in their huts and their bodies simply decayed there. By September, when the epidemic eased, disease had probably claimed ten people for every one who had died of actual starvation.

The peasants had nothing left but their mud huts and patches of potato ground, and they feared losing these, too, through eviction. Some kind landlords reduced the rents or canceled them altogether; but others, themselves ruined by unpaid rents, evicted tenants. In a typical eviction:

> The sheriff, a strong force of police, and . . . the crowbar brigade . . . were present. At a signal from

> the sheriff the work began. The miserable inmates of the cabins were dragged out upon the road; the thatched roofs were torn down and the earthen walls battered in by crowbars . . .; the screaming women, the half-naked children, the paralysed grandmother and the tottering grandfather were hauled out.[7]

The dazed family would sleep the first night under straw in the ruins of the tumbled cabin. Next day the troops would knock down any remains and drive the wailing tenants off the land. Then the evicted made huts by roofing ditches and bog holes with sticks and pieces of turf. Here whole families huddled together for shelter beside the road or on a hillside.

Desperately, the haggard peasants searched for work, but the only jobs to be had in Skibbereen were on the public works. Normally, the peasants had remained inside by their fires in winter. Now they had to go out in their rags, braving icy wind and snow to labor on the roads. Wages that year were still only eightpence a day. Women and children returning home from market sobbed with frustration at the single meal's worth of oatmeal or turnip they had been able to buy.

The situation grew more desperate as the British government began closing the public works. To the government the works had been a failure—they had been enormously expensive to run; they had bred corruption and violence; and the work had not been done efficiently. Nevertheless, their closing added to the misery. Although the market at Skibbereen was supplied

As an eviction force nears, neighbors sound an alarm.

with meat, bread, vegetables, and a new shipment of Indian corn, laborers turned off the public works no longer had the few pennies needed to buy them. People continued to starve. Not a scrap of seaweed remained on the beaches; it had all been picked for food.

Instead of supporting public works, the government began helping charitable organizations to distribute free soup and set up some soup kitchens of its own. If the peasants were given a minimum of food to eat, the government reasoned, this would free them during the day to plant potatoes on their own plots or work for farmers to prepare for the next harvest.

Each hungry peasant had to bring a bowl to a depot and stand in line until his turn came to have soup ladled into it. The daily ration consisted of "one pound of biscuit, meal or flour, or one quart of soup, thickened with

Neighbors rush to dig up an evicted tenant's potatoes.

meal, and four ounces of bread or biscuit."[8] Standing in line for soup humiliated the people of Skibbereen; but the alternative was starvation. Soup kitchens prevented them from starving to death but not from suffering extreme hunger. Watery soup was "no working food for people accustomed to fourteen pounds of potatoes daily."[9]

Unfortunately, the opening of soup kitchens and the closing of public works came too late for the peasants to plant many potatoes. Hunger left the peasants too weak to manure fields, dig drainage trenches, or prepare beds, and when a field was ready there were few seed potatoes available to plant. Although the planting was small, the summer of 1847 promised well with its clear, sunny weather, and there was not a trace of blight. In expectation of a good harvest, the government and the various agencies closed down their soup kitchens. The optimism and cheerfulness that had been absent for many months returned to the countryside. The harvest was healthy, but it was soon apparent that the small potato crop would not feed the people for a whole year.

Autumn passed and winter began. The winter of 1847-48 brought almost as much suffering as the previous one. Farmers with five to ten acres of land went hungry. Fever raged again. Dead bodies lay by roadsides and in fields. Skeleton-like beggars, tramped miles into Skibbereen, hoping to be committed to the jail or workhouse where they would get some food and clothing. When the government did not reopen either the public works or their soup kitchens, people grew more discontented than ever with British rule.

FLIGHT

With famine conditions growing worse, many began to see only one solution—to leave Ireland. Before the famine, only a few farmers had ever left Skibbereen. Though the potato failed from time to time, most peasants clung to their land. To leave one of the most beautiful countries in the world was difficult. But now the land they loved seemed cursed, and many felt it would never recover.

They looked to America for their refuge. Corn from America had eased their hunger. Relief ships from America and packages from Irishmen living there had brought them food and clothing. Letters from relatives and friends already in America were read aloud to groups of neighbors eager to listen. The letters told of high wages impossible in Ireland, of cheap land and large farms, of meals served every day as good as those eaten only on holidays in Skibbereen. An Irish folk song that mentioned letters from America said:

They say there's bread and work for all,
And the sun shines always there.[10]

Many letters contained money, while others held prepaid tickets for ship passage to New York or Boston. A husband in America sent for his wife and children, a son sent for his parents, a brother sent for his sister.

Almost no one wanted to emigrate to England or to British North America (Canada today) because of the strong hatred for the British. Yet sometimes they had to. Passage to New York or Boston cost more than a farmer or cottier could earn in a year. Only if he had saved carefully, hiding his coins in the thatch of his cabin, or if he had received money from America, could he afford to go there. Passage to England or British North America was considerably cheaper.

The first famine emigrants to go to America were the comfortable farmers who, encouraged by letters, had been debating for years whether or not to leave Ireland. With the first poor potato crop in 1845, they resolved to leave the following spring before famine and poverty engulfed them. They did so, departing during the spring and summer of 1846 as soon as the winter storms over the Atlantic ceased and emigrant ships resumed their traffic.

It was while these first emigrants were leaving that

peasants were discovering the wizened potatoes of a second ruined crop. People who previously had no thought of leaving faced a choice between flight and death. To afford passage, small farmers hurriedly sold their pigs and chickens, pots and spades, bedding, stools, and benches. Some begged for money.

Families and neighbors from Skibbereen walked to Cork, a seaport forty-two miles to the northeast. Most of the wayfarers carried their meager belongings on their shoulders. A few pushed carts. From Cork, some took boats to Liverpool in England. There the poorest would look for work, and those who could afford it would buy tickets on a packet sailing to America. Many simply camped in confusion on the quay at Cork, waiting for a chance American or Canadian schooner to land its load of grain in Cork harbor. Then they would bargain with the captain and set out with him.

During the winter of 1846-47, emigrant ships crossed the Atlantic throughout the stormy months for the first time. As the winter passed into spring and the horror of fever was added to starvation, the number leaving Skibbereen doubled. This was no carefully planned departure. The emigration of famine victims from Skibbereen was a hysterical flight from hunger and disease. Most left without food for a voyage that could take as long as eight weeks. Fever followed them across the Atlantic, killing many in the holds of the over-crowded "coffin ships" and still more after they reached American shores.

The poorest emigrants were cottiers and small farmers whose landlords paid their passage rather than evict them. Although this sounds like an act of kindness on the part of the landlords, it was one of economy. Paying a tenant's way to America cost a landlord less than paying the taxes demanded of him to support a tenant in the workhouse. Furthermore, pushing out the poorest tenants would clear a landlord's overly subdivided land for more efficient farming in the future. Many tenants, however, would not leave Ireland even if their way were paid.

Those who remained in Skibbereen watched snow fall during February 1848 and believed it would prevent the blight from reappearing. In a last desperate effort to buy seed to plant, they sold all they had left. Confidently, they planted about twice as many potatoes as the year before. Suddenly in June, fair weather turned to rain. In the middle of July, potato plants again blackened overnight. Another bad year was certain. The second complete failure in four years of inadequate crops devastated these already famished peasants.

By this time, few cottiers remained on the land. They had either died, been admitted to the workhouse, or fled to England or North America. There were farmers left, but they could no longer afford passage out of Ireland. And landlords could not get together the money to pay passage for their pauper tenants. After so much hardship, only those left among the farmers who had once been well off could raise the price of passage. These emigrants of 1848 were more skilled and better educated than the poorer farmers and cottiers who fled in 1847. They were accompanied by another normally more fortunate group, the shopkeepers. Since people were spending money on nothing except food, makers of cheap clothing, shoemakers, masons, carpenters, and tradesmen were forced to close their shops and leave. Twice as many Irishmen sailed to America in 1848 as the year before. And for the first time, more went to the United States than to Canada.

Over a million Irish crossed the Atlantic during the famine years. Many who went first to Canada later made their way across the border and moved south into New England. By 1848, over a quarter of the people of Skibbereen had died or emigrated. Most of those who fled to America did not have the money to travel beyond the port cities where they landed, usually New York or Boston. The few who possessed the cash that would have taken them to smaller towns or farm lands chose not to go. They lacked the experience for America's mechanized farming and did not want to lead isolated lives in the country, anyway. The shopkeepers and tradesmen of Skibbereen's single main street and market square joined cottiers and farmers from the town's blighted fields in the fastest-growing cities of the eastern United States.

FROM TYRANNY

Berlin, Prussia, 1848-1849

NOBLES, MIDDLE CLASS, AND WORKERS

The workday began early in Berlin. At four in the morning, the watchman announced the end of the night. Washerwomen, wearing flapping bonnets and cotton aprons, carried small lanterns to light their way to work. Workers for the gas companies climbed their ladders and turned out the street lamps. An hour or two later, peasant women from nearby villages flocked into town with their wooden carts full of milk, cheese, eggs, potatoes, and vegetables. Horses drew the big carts, and dogs pulled the small ones. The bakers' delivery boys pushed their rattling carts which carried daily bread to the people of the neighborhoods.

By seven, everyone in the city was eating his breakfast roll and drinking his morning coffee. Doors opened, and workmen left for work. Laborers headed for the iron foundry, brandy distilleries, and wool spinning mills. Weavers began to operate their looms, and shopkeepers opened their shops. Doctors and lawyers, merchants and journalists left for their offices. Students and professors headed for the university. Children left for school. Women began their housework.

Different classes of people in Berlin lived in different sections of the city. Rich and poor were strangers to one another, even though they passed each other in the street and in the public squares and parks. At noontime and on Sundays, the various classes mingled as they walked about on Unter-den-Linden (Under-the-Limes), the most magnificent street in Berlin. It boasted splendid public buildings, the best hotels and restaurants in Berlin, and a number of confectioners and wine shops. A double row of lime and chestnut trees, enclosing a green promenade, ran up the middle of this wide avenue.

Berlin was the capital of Prussia and the home of its king, Frederick William IV, who believed his right to rule came from God. He shared this right with no one, not even his nobles. The few nobles who lived in Berlin were allowed to serve only as government officials who carried out his will or as officers in his army. There was no single, large country of Germany in 1848; Prussia was the strongest of over thirty rival German-speaking states. Each small, separate state had its own system of money, postage, and weights, its own laws and its own ruler.

Some fifteen thousand Prussian soldiers were permanently garrisoned in Berlin, and they gave the city a military air. Dressed in blue uniforms and spiked helmets, soldiers drilled in the squares, guarded the public buildings, shouted commands at the people of the city, hustled all but the nobles into their houses every night at ten o'clock, and broke up meetings where they feared people might criticize the king. As a result, the people of the middle and working classes had come to hate the soldiers.

Members of the middle class of Berlin earned more money than anyone else, but they had no part in the government. They were the doctors, lawyers, bankers, and industrialists; teachers, professors, and journalists; innkeepers, merchants, and dealers in wool, flax, grain, and liquor. Many had studied at the University of Berlin, but others had not attended classes since their fourteenth year, when they completed the gymnasium course of Latin, Greek, French, mathematics, history and geography, literature, Bible studies, and a smattering of chemistry and physics.

Though members of the middle class were wealthy, they were not ashamed of living more cheaply than they might in order to save money. Instead of renting a whole house, a family leased a four- or five-room apartment. A typical flat had

> high, cheerful rooms, with painted ceilings, light curtains, many objects of Bohemian glass-ware, and vases of flowers scattered around; but no carpet on the polished parquette floor, and no heavy articles of furniture. [1]

The furnishings were simple—a sofa, a desk, some plain wooden chairs, bookcases, and a table or two. There were candlestands and shaded lamps, music holders, and pianos. Inexpensive sketches or engravings hung on the walls.

Prussians cheer Frederick William IV in the early 1840's.

Although middle-class families spent little on mere luxury, they spent money readily on entertainment. During the winter, they often attended the theater or opera or went to a dance in the home of friends. Berliners went skating in the park or visited the art gallery on Sundays. Tea parties in each other's homes were popular among married couples. Summer brought outdoor concerts to Berlin. On Friday afternoons and Sunday mornings especially, people sat at tables in the coffee gardens just outside the city. They ordered cups of coffee or mugs of beer and listened to music. On Sundays and holidays, families took picnics to parks outside the city.

These families ate well. A little before noon the housewife spread a white cloth over the dining table for her husband and children, who came home for lunch. They all sat down to a midday meal of wurst, tongue, or some other cold meat, black bread and butter, preserves and fruit, and light wine or beer. When the family had gone, the wife cleared up the luncheon table and prepared for dinner, the main meal of the day, which usually came about six o'clock, after the business day ended. A soup course preceded the roast meat served with sauerkraut or some other vegetable, preserves, and pickled fruit. Sometimes a salad followed, perhaps cold potatoes with vinegar and anchovies added for zest. Pudding or fruit appeared for dessert, and black rye bread with butter or cheese ended the meal. Berliners drank light wine with their dinner, and strong black coffee afterwards. Before going to bed, families sat down to a fourth meal, a supper of cold meat, potato salad, fruit, and wine or beer.

Across the river Spree from the Linden quarter lived the poorest workers of Berlin:

> A gulf yawned between the porcelain elegance of the wide street under the linden trees with the elegant carriages enamelled in various colours . . .

> and . . . the terrible blocks of slum tenements in the North of the city where the poor cloth weavers lived. [2]

Factory workers, apprentices, and servants lived alongside the cloth weavers. Badly paved and dirty streets led to the outskirts of Berlin and the barren sandy plain on which the city stood. In the slum, families of five or six or more lived crammed together in a single room, often with such a low ceiling that the adults could barely stand up straight. Sometimes the floor was uneven, and water ran down the damp walls. If the few small windows had broken panes, as was often the case, they were simply pasted over with paper or stuffed with straw which further reduced the light in an already dim room. The room contained a black iron stove, some old pots and cooking utensils, a table and a few wooden stools. A washtub sat on one of the stools. The entire family slept in one large bed that was made of hard boards covered only with some moldy straw and a few rags.

Workers' families had no luxuries. The poorest ate little besides potatoes but most were able to afford bread, herring, sausages, and beer—the cheapest foods. Women made their family's linen clothes, starting from flax. Often men and women wore their outfits both winter and summer. Men wore rough blouses and coarse, close-fitting trousers. Women wore long-sleeved blouses and ankle-length skirts, adding woolen shawls in winter. Some had a single good suit or dress for Sundays.

About half of the workers of Berlin were skilled craftsmen and belonged to the so-called middle class. At this time, however, Berlin had more of these weavers, tailors, shoemakers, tanners, and carpenters than it needed. Most of them were no better off than factory workers, although they had higher status.

Industrialization had only recently come to Berlin, but over a tenth of its more than four hundred thousand inhabitants already worked in factories. Men and women spent between twelve and eighteen hours a day at their machines, six and sometimes seven days a week. They

Factory workers take a short break to eat their lunches.

molded iron, spun flax, or wove wool, linen, or cotton cloth. Children under the age of nine were forbidden to work, but once they reached their ninth birthdays, they, too, went into the factories. Their work schedule was kept "short"—ten hours a day until the sixteenth birthday. This was supposed to give them time to go to school, but many workers' children never got there.

The machine age had put various people out of work. Many spinners and handloom weavers who had worked in their own homes were forced out of business by the spinning machines and steam-powered looms of the recently established factories. New railroads left wagon drivers without jobs, river steamers deprived boatmen of their earnings. Factory workers, the poorer craftsmen, and the unemployed often had to beg or steal in order to eat. Some received money, food, and land for raising potatoes from the city government.

Sometimes workers, poor craftsmen, and the jobless attended evening meetings where they listened avidly to speeches given by educated and traveled men who devoted themselves to the service of the working class and called themselves socialists. In every country of the world, these socialist speakers asserted, the middle class was the enemy of the workers; they urged the Berlin workers to unite and demand higher wages, shorter working hours, and more schooling. Some socialists encouraged the workers to look for chances to revolt against the middle and upper classes. They claimed that eventually workers would gain wealth and power and become rulers themselves.

The workers of Berlin were not yet ready to join together in a fight for rights, but the socialist leaders tried to make use of any spontaneous rioting that might occur. Such a time came in the spring of 1847. Meager potato and grain harvests since 1845 had made food scarce in the markets and this scarcity, in turn, had raised the prices of potatoes and bread. High food prices enraged the poor, and they accused the middle-class shopkeepers of cheating them. Some of them went so far as to put their discontent into action.

In April 1847, a number of women raided the markets and food shops. Other poor women, impoverished craftsmen, and vagabonds joined them, and socialist leaders urged them on. They strode round the city, "whistling, roaring, shrieking, singing, and uttering noises of every kind."[3] In the market places, the crowd scattered hucksters' potatoes and vegetables into the street. They cleaned the food out of the butchers' and grocers' shops but hurt no other property providing the owner meekly allowed himself to be robbed. If a shopkeeper resisted the raid, "his windows were broken, everything smashable was smashed, and he himself [was] beaten black and blue."[4] In bakers' shops, the women weighed the loaves. If the bread were the advertised weight, they congratulated the baker for his honesty. Then the women wrote a notice in chalk on his door saying he was to be trusted and not to be robbed.

By the fourth day, when the food riots had spread through many of the streets, the soldiers were sent in to clear the streets and arrest the noisiest demonstrators. The workers hated the soldiers more than ever for their part in breaking up the demonstrations and imprisoning

During German food riots, citizens attacked market vendors.

a hundred people. The middle and upper classes looked to the soldiers to re-establish order. Only after the troops had brought the rioting under control, did the frightened middle- and upper-class citizens dare to venture into the public squares again.

MIDDLE-CLASS DISSATISFACTION

Members of the middle class had enough to eat. They lived in decent houses, and they had money to spare for education and entertainment, but they had one great unsatisfied desire. They wanted to change the system of government under which they were living. For years, they had been asking their king to give them a part in the government. They wanted a constitution guaranteeing that every middle-class man could vote in regular elections. These men would elect a prime minister to govern Prussia and an assembly of representatives to make laws. They also wanted free education, a reduction in the size of the army, and a decrease in taxes.

Well-educated members of the middle class wanted still more. They wanted the king of Prussia to unite the thirty-odd German states into a single nation. The people of these states had a common culture. Nearly all spoke German, and the works of German-speaking philosophers, poets, and musicians were acclaimed by German-speaking people, regardless of the state in which the artists lived. For years, practical Prussian businessmen had hoped for a united Germany. They knew that one system of laws, money, and postage would make trading easier between states and would be good for business.

Many members of the middle class wanted freedom of the press and freedom to hold meetings so they could spread their ideas. Students of the University of Berlin grew more excited than anybody about the changes in government that the middle class desired. Enthusiastically, they discussed popular government, and even German unification, among themselves and with their professors.

King Frederick William IV, confident that God stood behind him, refused to make changes. He knew that an elected prime minister and assembly for Prussia would decrease his power, as would a united Germany—unless he were its leader, and he could not be sure he would be chosen. To maintain his power, he made certain that the army and the police broke up public meetings and kept watch over the University of Berlin. If a professor was caught urging government by the people, he lost his job. If the police suspected anyone, they searched his house and read his letters; if they found anything to indicate that a man's opinions differed from the king's, they arrested him. Newspapers that criticized the king were banned; pamphlets were often censored.

This treatment made the middle classes and the students more angry. Their determination worried Frederick William. Trusting in the likelihood that he would be king of a united Germany, Frederick William lifted his ban on discussion of unification in order to quiet the anger of the people. He agreed to let newspapers print opinions about unification. Scholars and lawyers took heart and resumed their discussions of a wider Germany. Professors once again dared to urge unification in the lecture rooms, and journalists pleaded for it in the newspapers. But the reformers were still arrested if they mentioned an elected government or a free press.

Leaders of the movement felt that some day the people would actually have to fight for their other demands since the king would not grant them. Inside their jackets, many members of the middle-class movement wore the black, red, and gold flag that was the symbol of a united Germany and of democratic revolution. Content for a time with showing their affiliation in this milder way, they waited for their chance to force a change.

THE MARCH REVOLUTION AND ITS AFTERMATH

Spring came early to Berlin in 1848, and by late February the evenings were as warm as May. On February 28, Unter-den-Linden was crowded with people, as usual. But their pleasant strolling had stopped. Small groups of men gathered to talk of a startling event. When soldiers passed, they scattered or spoke more quietly; then they came together again. From hour to hour, more people gathered to hear or tell the news. One man told another: "The King of France has fled Paris; the people of Paris have set up a free Republic of France."

Berliners greeted the news with great excitement because they felt something similar must happen soon in their city. University students were so exhilarated that they left their studies and rushed out to the squares. One student later wrote that in order to quiet his blood he had found it necessary to walk until he was exhausted.

For many evenings after that, students and middle-class citizens by the thousands congregated in the cafés in the park along the river Spree. A bandstand stood in the open space, and on fine evenings concerts were given. While vendors sold beer and cherry brandy, cucumbers in vinegar, and sausages, citizens began to talk over changes for their own government. After many meetings, six thousand citizens signed a petition to the king. They asked him to withdraw the troops from Berlin, to grant freedom of the press, free speech, and the right of free assembly; they asked him to summon the diet, an assembly which represented the nobility of Prussia, and direct it to write a more democratic constitution for Prussia.

Meanwhile, Frederick William IV had received numerous petitions from all over Prussia making similar requests. He disregarded these as well as the one signed by the citizens of Berlin. The impassioned petitions that small groups of citizens continued to deliver sounded more and more urgent. Evening crowds in the parks and squares of Berlin grew larger. The people became hard to control, and two of them died in scuffles with the troops. For the first time, Berliners whistled and hooted at the soldiers who had been driving them off the streets and ordering them around for years. The people even

Medical students plot the overthrow of the government.

talked about forcing the soldiers to leave the city. And the troops, who had always had the upper hand, began to feel insecure.

On March 18, mobs of middle- and working-class citizens crowded the palace square, demanding a constitution and withdrawal of the troops. Finally the king gave in, and from the palace balcony, one of his officials read this proclamation:

> It is the King's will that the Press shall be free;
> It is the King's will that the Diet be summoned at once;
> It is the King's will that there shall be a Constitution on the most liberal basis to include all German countries;
> It is the King's will that there shall be a German National Flag;
> It is the King's will that all Customs barriers shall be done away with in Germany;
> It is the King's will that Prussia shall place herself at the head of the movement. [5]

The people were overjoyed. Larger crowds collected in the square near the palace to cheer the king. An eyewitness described their reaction:

> People of the most highly educated classes jumped up on vehicles in order to spread the good news. . . . I saw people embracing each other and crying for joy; women at the windows waved handkerchiefs; materials for bonfires in the evening were carried through the streets. . . . Collections for the poor were made as a token of rejoicing. [6]

Wanting to break up the mob, the king ordered troops to clear the palace square. Foot soldiers marched directly into the square, and soldiers on horseback trotted into the rejoicing crowd with drawn swords. A catastrophe followed. Two mysterious shots rang out, hurting no one but terrifying the people. Their joyous hurrahs changed to cries of fury against the king, who, they believed, had turned the troops against them. "We are betrayed! We are betrayed," they cried. And then, "To arms! To arms! [7]

Almost immediately, barricades began to rise in the center of Berlin. People gathered at every street corner to build them. The first barricade consisted of two hackney coaches, a carriage, a sentry box, pieces of curbing, and some barrels. A fruit stall made up another. Omnibuses and carts laden with bricks and timber were particularly welcome. Postal and brewery cars were overturned. Oil barrels were stacked on top of each other and lamp posts, stones, and dirt were piled on top of them. Pavements were torn up, and boards bridging the gutters were removed. Together workmen in worn shirts and well-dressed gentlemen dragged scaffolding poles and beams. Even women and children helped. They brought beds, furniture, and sacks of flour from their houses, as well as doors, gates, and fences.

The troops set out against the barricades. Fierce fighting continued throughout the night. Students, teachers, lawyers, and tradesmen gave the orders. But servants, apprentices, and factory workers fought next to them on

Berliners fight soldiers from barricades and windows.

the barricades. Rich and poor united in the determination to drive the troops from the city.

Probably no more than a hundred students and several hundred others took part in the fighting, owing to the shortage of guns. But tens of thousands helped to build barricades and search for weapons, which included planks, clubs, pitchforks, and old rusty sabers as well as muskets and pistols borrowed from gun shops and theaters or taken from soldiers' quarters. Boys helped to mold bullets and forge lance tips in the streets. They even loaded small brass cannon with marbles. Women carried sandwiches and coffee out to the barricade fighters and sheltered the wounded.

The people attacked the soldiers from the roofs of houses as well as from the barricades. Sharpshooters kept up well-aimed fire from rooftops. Pavement stones and roof tiles were hurled down. Boiling oil was poured from open windows onto the troops. People set fire to the sentry boxes near the city gates, and the red glow of the flames could be seen across the city. All night long the troops fired their cannon at the barricades and the houses.

By morning, 230 civilians and twenty soldiers had been killed. The army was exhausted but still there; the people refused to abandon the barricades until the troops left town. Once again the king gave in to the people's demands. He ordered the soldiers to withdraw to Potsdam, about fifteen miles west of Berlin. Only when the troops left the city did the shooting stop.

In the days that followed, the king rode on horseback through the streets of Berlin carrying the new black, red, and gold flag that symbolized a united Germany instead of the old black and white flag of Prussia. He agreed to let the people elect an assembly to draw up a constitution for Prussia, although he did not say he would accept it. And he promised to urge the princes of the various German states to unite. The tricolor flag of the Revolution flew above the palace in Berlin, and the citizens wrote on all the public buildings "The People's Property." The people of Berlin thought they were victorious. They had the king's promises for reform, and they had already forced the troops out of the city. The citizens' militia was guarding the public buildings, and there were no more army officers left to censor articles or break up meetings.

In the streets, people talked freely and enjoyed not being ordered around. Revolutionary leaders wrote whatever pamphlets and newspaper articles they wanted. Huge placards pasted on walls all over the city demanded that the people soon have a share in the government.

Political clubs were formed. Supporters of the Revolution spoke to the men and women of Berlin at evening meetings and joined in discussions afterward over mugs of beer or decanters of wine. But only one out of twenty Berliners attended these meetings. The rest of the people showed less interest in the Revolution. Many working- and middle-class citizens even remained loyal to the king, who had left the city within a week after the night of the Revolution.

Although middle-class citizens and workers had fought together against the troops at the barricades, they realized shortly afterward that they had been fighting for different reasons. The middle class wanted freedom of the press, a constitution for Prussia, and a united Germany. The workers knew that these things would not help them at all; they wanted higher wages and a shorter, ten-hour, working day. They wanted free schools and lower rents. They wanted money for men who lost their jobs to machines. The middle-class revolutionaries began to fear the workers and the workers to distrust the middle class. Only a few days after the fighting ended, middle-class citizens began talking of the workers as "rabble." They feared that the workers would decide to fight against the middle class, too. To prevent the workers from acquiring guns, the middle class excluded them from the citizens' militia.

More and more Berliners now began to agree that the city needed real soldiers to control the mass meetings of the workers and enforce quiet. When some troops came back to Berlin at the end of March, joyful citizens crowned one regiment with garlands. The return of these soldiers, however, was not enough to stop a crowd of angry workers from storming the Berlin Arsenal one night and helping themselves to guns.

Early in November 1848, the rest of the troops returned to Berlin on command of the king's general. Most citizens were now glad to see the soldiers. They did not fight back as the troops took complete control of the city. First, the army disbanded the citizens' militia and collected the rifles that the revolutionaries had been carrying. Then soldiers ordered persons who were not citizens of Berlin to leave the city within twenty-four hours. Next they closed the political clubs and forbade meetings in streets and other public places. No more than twenty people were allowed to gather in the daytime; no more than ten by night. Police authorities prohibited the printing of papers, pamphlets, and posters that they did not approve. Order returned to Berlin but tyranny had come back with it.

Meanwhile, Frederick William allowed people everywhere in Prussia to elect representatives to gather in Berlin and draw up a constitution. Craftsmen, teachers, lawyers, editors, journalists, and other revolutionaries arrived at the assembly hall. They began to prepare a constitution for Prussia, but they had difficulty agreeing on what they wanted it to say.

The king's conservative advisers convinced him that

the Assembly was becoming too radical and that armies ruled better than elected diets ever could. When the Assembly finally questioned whether Frederick William's right to rule was actually given to him by God, the king became enraged and ended the meetings. He replaced the Assembly's partly written constitution with a less radical one of his own. His constitution did permit the people of Prussia to elect a diet which would represent more of the people than before, but the richer people would be entitled to the most representatives. Actually, the new diet had very little power; all it could do without risking the king's veto was to reject new taxes. Nevertheless, the middle class was pleased to have representatives for the first time and to see censorship of letters and of the press decreased. The workers, on the other hand, got none of the reforms they wanted.

When their own Revolution collapsed, citizens of Berlin turned their hopes to Frankfurt, where an assembly of delegates from all the German-speaking states was writing a constitution to unite the states into a nation. Immediately after the Revolution in Berlin, the governments of the thirty-odd states, frightened by the threat of further revolution, had agreed to let their citizens choose the delegates. The assembly delegates all had good ideas, but, since they had never been politicians, they had difficulty translating their ideas into practical measures.

After months of debate, the Frankfurt Assembly finished its constitution in March 1849. The delegates determined that Prussia should stand at the head of a united Germany, and they voted to make Frederick William IV the new nation's emperor. He refused to accept a crown from the common people; only princes were fit to bestow such honors. He called the Frankfurt Parliament's offer "a fictitious coronet baked out of mire and clay." [8]

When Frederick William rejected the crown, other German princes turned their backs on the constitution drawn up at Frankfurt. The work of the assembly was ruined. Disillusioned delegates left Frankfurt knowing their constitution would never be put into effect. Berliners had been disappointed at their failure to reform the single state of Prussia; failure to unite the German states added to their frustration. Their Revolution had failed completely. Many were convinced that it was hopeless to dream of reforming and unifying Germany.

REPRESSION AND ESCAPE

After 1848, life in Berlin became more restricted. The censors were everywhere. Radical newspapers were silenced. School children were taught that a king could govern a state better than elected amateurs. Hunts for the barricade fighters and leaders of the political clubs went on for months, even years. Police read letters, searched homes, and arrested suspects. No one was executed, but many faced eight to twenty years in military prisons.

Gradually, citizens decided to leave Berlin. Some fled to evade imprisonment or left after serving their sentences; others wanted to escape the endless restrictions that the government imposed; a few actually broke out of prison. Germans who had participated in the Revolution, and who left their homes as a result, were called

"Forty-eighters." They came from all classes and from every trade and profession.

Some Forty-eighters went to Switzerland, others to France, still others to England, and more to America. Between 1848 and 1853 nearly a thousand people left Berlin for America. America represented everything the Forty-eighters had tried to win for their own land. Patriots who had dreamed of unifying Germany wanted to go to a country they knew was already unified. Revolutionaries who had fought for a constitution and personal freedom wanted to go to a country where they understood they could vote, write, and speak as they wished. Discontented factory workers who had no land of their own and poor craftsmen who had no work wanted to go to a country they had heard offered cheap land and plenty of jobs.

While these families were leaving Berlin, other Forty-eighters were leaving cities in other German states. Revolutions similar to the one in Berlin had started and failed during 1848 and 1849 in almost every German princedom. Some Forty-eighters received money from relatives, friends, or German societies in America. Many hoped to return to their homes some day, but few ever did.

Forty-eighters were not the only Germans emigrating to America during these years. They joined a larger movement of a hundred thousand men, women, and children who left in the 1850's. These people came from country districts, especially in the southern and western German states. Most of them were farmers, village shopkeepers, and craftsmen who knew little about politics and had played no part in any revolution. Yet they, too, were dissatisfied. The farmers among them complained of having too little land. They had suffered from potato rot in 1845 and 1846, and many fell deeply into debt. Poor grain harvests added to the food shortage and caused food prices to shoot upwards. Village shopkeepers could not afford the high food prices, either. Craftsmen left their villages because they hated the high food prices and the new machines. Factories were making shoes, clothes, and furniture more cheaply than any handicraftsman could. Many shoemakers, household weavers, and carpenters had gone bankrupt.

Germans who came to America frequently followed a water route. Many took a boat along the Elbe River to Hamburg or along the Weser River to Bremen. At these ports, they booked passage on ships that had unloaded cargoes of cotton from New Orleans or tobacco from Baltimore and were bound homeward for those ports; empty timber ships also offered them accommodations on a return trip to New York. Most of them came with enough money to move away from the cities where they landed. Some continued their journey from New Orleans by steamboat up the Mississippi River; many who had landed in the northeast traveled to Albany to follow the Erie Canal to Buffalo and across the Great Lakes to Chicago. German immigrants spread all over the United States, but especially throughout the Middle West. Most of the farmers and craftsmen among them sought out rural surroundings similar to those they had come from, while the middle-class Forty-eighters tended to make their homes in the German-speaking communities of the larger cities.

FROM DISORDER

En-p'ing, China, 1860's

THE FAMILY, A FORCE FOR ORDER

From one of the higher hilltops in the Pearl River Delta in South China in the 1860's, one would have seen the muddy branches of the river and the hundreds of creeks and canals that criss-crossed the rolling plains at the edge of the sea. Thousands of junks, sampans, bamboo rafts, and fishing boats made their way over the crowded waters that linked the towns and villages of the delta. Terraced farmlands cut into the hillsides, and cultivated fields filled every available bit of space in the valleys, making the land look as crowded as the waterways. The brown tones of treeless hills, muddy waters, and sunbaked mud houses dominated the scene. Only the fresh green of rice plants brought brightness to the land.

As far as the eye could see, large market towns were surrounded by ten or twenty little farming villages. Walls of piled stones or of sunbaked mud brick encircled most of the towns and villages, but in many places the walls were broken and scars of war showed plainly. There were other signs of trouble. Here and there a village was reduced to a pile of ashes and rubble. Riverside embankments, built to keep the rising river in its course, were flattened where they had not held strong against the torrent of floodwaters. And, on closer look, the people of the delta appeared thin and ragged.

In the midst of this troubled scene, the Chinese family stood as a force for order. To the Chinese, the family was not just a group of related people, but also that group's land and house, their animals, and even their reputation. Every man, woman, and child worked for the family. The peasant who sold extra rice, the craftsman who wove straw baskets, the girl who made incense sticks or gathered shellfish, all pooled their earnings with the rest of the family.

Men fill the street of a busy market in the Pearl Delta.

A family lived together, usually three generations of it. When the sons married, they brought their wives home. This meant many people sleeping under the same roof, but usually the family bedroom would be partitioned into units for each son's family, and the older children, or perhaps the grandparents, would sleep in the living room. Sometimes, when there were many sons, they would divide the family property and set up separate homes.

As a peasant farmer and his young sons rose at dawn in the market town of En-p'ing, they could see the morning light coming through the white paper that covered the window of the bedroom in their house. In dressing themselves, they had only to attach their leather or straw sandals or slip into their wooden clogs, since most Chinese were too poor to own more than one set of clothes, and these were worn both night and day. Men, women, and children dressed alike, in wide trousers and loose-fitting, blue cotton jackets that buttoned down the front. In winter, they added quilted jackets, or if they had none, they stuffed loose wads of cotton between the layers of their summer clothes. If it were summer, a season of hot sun but frequent rain, the peasant farmer and his sons would plan to wear their broad-brimmed, straw hats that provided shade and their cloaks of dried rush leaves that shed the water.

As the men and boys moved from the bedroom through the kitchen to the living room, they walked on pounded earth covered with grass mats. Light spilled into the living room from around the edges of the thick mat that hung at the front doorway, reaching from the roof to the ground. One of the boys might roll the matting up under the roof where it hung on warm days.

In the small kitchen, between the two rooms, the wife or wives, supervised by their mother-in-law and helped by the older daughters, were already busy at a simple stove made of a few bricks piled to keep burning leaves, charcoal, or bamboo branches in place. In a niche above the stove hung a piece of red paper—red was lucky—inscribed with the name of the kitchen god. In good weather, women cooked in the yard, since the kitchen was tiny. It was too small to hold the storage bins, and one of the daughters would have to go into the living room to dip into a large reed mat twisted into the shape of a great jar and bring a bowlful of rice back to the stove. Another would reach up to a string of dried onions hanging from the rafters for something to add to the pot of greens being simmered to flavor the rice. The women prepared raw or pickled vegetables, bean curd or dried fish and, always, tea. Sometimes they had to flavor their dishes strongly enough to cover the taste of rice that had gone sour and which they were too poor to throw out. Rice was the main dish for three meals a day; poor families tasted meat, fresh fish, and eggs only on special occasions.

After breakfast, the peasant farmer and his sons walked through their poor residential district at the edge of town out to the small garden plots on the terraced hillsides. In these plots, rented from richer townsmen, they grew cabbages and soybeans, sweet potatoes, peanuts, and cotton. The rice fields lay beyond the gardens, in the lowland. Two acres of rice could support a whole family for a year. Many plots were smaller, though, running down to fractions of an acre. Women and children planted rice seeds on the hillsides while men and older boys did the heavier work of driving water buffalo to plow the low-lying fields, hoeing the earth by hand, and spreading human and animal excrement or soybean cakes to fertilize it. When the seeds on the hillsides had sprouted, boys painstakingly transplanted a handful of shoots at a time to the fields below. Since rice shoots grow only in very wet soil, the peasants had to spend their days slowly flooding the fields by treading small-sized irrigation wheels that dumped out bucketfuls of water from the irrigation canals. In this way, the whole field was kept under several inches of water. The peasants went on day after day, weeding and treading until the rice was ready for reaping.

The men and boys cut the ripe rice stalks and carried them home in bundles attached to poles balanced across their shoulders. In the yards beside their houses, the women beat the stalks against a frame of slats to detach the grain. A mill, turned by hand, removed the hull from the kernels of rice. After all this work, the peasants, too poor to own land, turned half the rice or more over to the landlords as rent for their plots on the hillsides and in the paddies.

If a peasant ever had extra rice or beans, eggs, chickens, fruit, or vegetables to sell, he and his sons would take these in to market. Following the unpaved road through their district of sun-dried mud-brick houses only seven feet high, a farmer and his sons would probably walk toward better and better houses until they came to

Peasants pedal an irrigation wheel to water the fields.

the handsome walled-in stone and wood homes of the rich merchants, moneylenders, and retired civil and military officers near the center of town. They passed the carpenter's shop with its freshly planed wood, the blacksmith's with its sounds of iron ringing against iron, and a few inns and teashops and stores from which came the familiar smells of cooking pork and burning incense.

On market days, the streets were so crowded that people had to push their way through mobs of bakers, fruit sellers, vendors of ornaments, shoemakers, and druggists who had all set up outdoor stalls. Countless hucksters walked back and forth with baskets and trays slung from carrying-poles across their shoulders. A peasant and his sons wielded chopsticks as they sampled hot food prepared before their eyes. They joined a group in a teahouse to hear a storyteller or to have their fortunes told. If they had collected enough copper coins from what they had sold, they visited the money changer to trade them for silver. The money changer's copper and silver coins, both with holes in the middle, hung on strings from a table set in the street. Nearby a barber had placed a chest of drawers as a seat for his customers. He would shave most of a peasant's head and braid the remaining hair into a single plait that fell behind. If the barber's own braid got in his way as he bent to shave a customer, he would wrap it around his neck.

Some of the farmers in the market were carrying baskets of mulberry shoots to sell to the owners of silkworms.

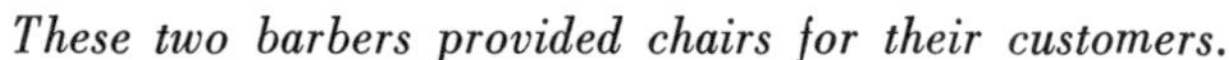

These two barbers provided chairs for their customers.

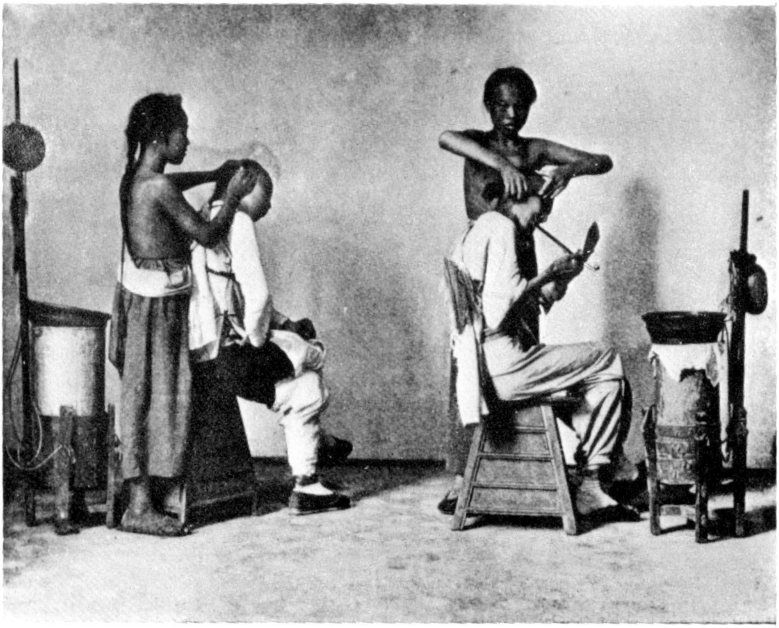

Mulberry trees needed dryness, and they grew on the hillsides where the men who raised them dug trenches and built fish ponds to drain any excess moisture from the soil. Women and children performed the lighter tasks of stripping the young shoots off the trees and packing them into baskets for market.

Some peasant women kept silkworms themselves and took the mulberry shoots home to feed to them. As the worms matured, they spun cocoons of silken thread. Women plunged the fully-formed cocoons into hot water to kill the worms and soften the natural gum that held the silk filaments together. Then they sat in their doorways patiently unwinding the gossamer threads and hanging them on frames to dry in the wind.

Many women in En-p'ing were confined to indoor or yard work because their feet had been bound, and they could not stand or walk for long. A girl's feet were tightly wrapped with long strips of cloth almost as soon as she began to walk, and this binding continued for the rest of her life. It prevented her feet from growing properly and curled her toes under with a most painful pressure. Though the pain would cease in time, her feet would remain abnormally shaped and unable to bear her weight easily. Bound feet were small and considered beautiful; they changed a woman's gait and posture as high heeled shoes do. The poorest peasants did not practice this custom because they needed the labor of their women and girls in the fields.

On a girl's wedding day, her father and mother turned their daughter over to a young man whom she had probably never met. The bride, bowing respectfully, would

Women work in their yard; one (center) reels silk threads.

bid her parents good-by—expecting to see them again only on special occasions—and go to live with her husband's family. Joining a new family was a difficult adjustment for the bride, who began following the orders of her mother-in-law and doing more housework than she had ever done before. It would have been useless for her to complain to her husband who, to be considered a faithful son and a good brother, had to take the side of his blood family in all disputes.

A bride was treated with greater respect and even smiled upon as soon as she bore a son. A son was treasured as an extra back to bend in the transplanting of rice, an extra pair of legs to tread the irrigation wheels, and as a male who would one day carry on the family. But when a girl was born, the family did not mask its disappointment. The poorest parents even killed their girl babies during very hard times, to reduce the number of mouths to feed.

If a father had many sons and could spare one or two from the fields and find the money for the lessons, he might send the smartest to school. They would have a chance to become merchants or scholars or government officials, rather than rice farmers. Schoolboys had to be at school as dawn broke, sitting in a crowded room and reciting aloud, sometimes screaming at the tops of their voices, passages from the ancient writings of Confucius and Mencius. When a boy felt he knew the passage he was working on by heart, he would recite it for his teacher. If his recitation was good, he would go on to learn another. He also practiced calligraphy, the writing of Chinese characters with a brush-pen and ink, and he studied counting and arithmetic with the abacus. This training was long and hard, and the few boys who completed it did not do so before they were twenty. The more sons a man had in school, the higher the status of his family in the town.

Both boys and girls learned at an early age to honor and respect their elders:

> I approached my grandfather with awe, my father and mother with veneration, and my elder brother with respect. I never spoke unless spoken to. . . .[1]

While the younger generations worked in the fields or in the household, the very old people relaxed in the warm sunshine and watched children spin tops, fly kites, play marbles or quiet games of ball.

When food was scarce, the last bowl of rice went to a hungry grandmother, rather than to a child, as is shown in the story of a Chinese man who said to his wife:

> We are so poor that we cannot even support mother. Moreover, the little one shares mother's food. Why not bury this child? We may have another; but, if mother should die, we cannot obtain her again. [2]

The wife dared not contradict her husband, who began to dig a grave for the child. Suddenly he discovered a vase full of gold—a reward from heaven for a son so faithful to his parents.

Veneration of one's parents and grandparents continued even after their deaths, for they remained members of the family. The Chinese believed that when a person died, his spirit went on living and had to be cared for. The dead needed the paper money and the paper clothes that the living burned for them. Burning turned the paper into spirit money and spirit clothes that the dead could use. These rituals bound the living and dead members of the family together.

Many Chinese believed that their dead ancestors possessed supernatural powers. If the spirits were happy with the services performed for them by the living, they would help answer prayers; but if the spirits of the dead were ignored, they wandered the world as ghosts and lost their power. Naturally, the living wanted to keep the spirits of their ancestors happy and strong so as to benefit from their help.

Every family, rich or poor, had a shrine that housed the spirits of its ancestors. The shrine occupied a special platform against the wall of the main room. It contained wooden tablets commemorating the parents of the head of the household and, if there was space enough, those of his less recent ancestors back to his great-great-grandparents. Each tablet showed the name, birth date, and age at death of the man or woman it commemorated and was sometimes carved with the figures of animals. Candlesticks, a vase of flowers, and incense burners stood in front of the tablets, as well as dishes of food that would eventually be eaten by the living members of the family.

When the head of the family set out food for the ancestors, he knelt on a straw cushion at the foot of the platform and led his family in prayers. Usually he prayed just for his own parents and grandparents, but a mention of his most remote ancestor meant that he remembered all those in between. Sons learned how to commemorate their ancestors from watching their fathers. When the father died, the eldest son would inherit the tablets. He would have a new tablet made to commemorate his father and when his mother died, one for her, too.

Spirits other than those of ancestors as well as various gods were also worshiped and petitioned for such benefits as abundant crops, prosperous shops, and good health. A mother might hurry to a temple, light incense to please a god, offer money, and pray that her child

A boy and two men join in a ritual at the family altar.

would recover from a sudden illness. Although the Chinese of the 1860's did not know it, they actually created many of the conditions that produced the diseases from which they suffered. Water was the symbol of money and so they left puddles undisturbed, allowing them to become breeding grounds for malarial mosquitoes. Women swept loose rubbish out of their doorways into a pile of decay that attracted flies which then lighted on food and brought disease. No one realized the value of draining sewage or of keeping clean and some ate unboiled food grown in fields fertilized with human excrement; few escaped the resulting dysentery and cholera. The Chinese walked over damp mud floors in bare feet or in shoes with thin cloth or paper soles and contracted rheumatism. They lived close together, ate from a common dish, and did not hesitate to spit; these practices spread tuberculosis among them.

Since many children died from disease, women bore almost twice as many offspring as they expected would live to adulthood. As new generations of children were born, more and more people shared the same ancestors. Though this group of relatives was larger than even the largest family, it too, clung together as a clan. To a clan belonged all the dead, living, and yet unborn members of an original family. After his family, a man's loyalty was to his clan.

THE CLAN AND THE FORCES FOR DISORDER

Sometimes a village consisted of the houses and streets and fields of only one clan. Other communities, like the market town of En-p'ing, sheltered members of several clans. Each clan lived in a separate section near its own ancestral hall, which housed spirits too many generations back to be worshiped in family shrines.

A clan provided for the welfare of its members. It owned a good deal of land, which it leased to poor kinsmen who would otherwise have had to hire out as day laborers. Clan members who had grown rich through trade lent or gave money to the sick and hungry, and supported schools to prepare the brightest boys for the Chinese civil service examinations. The oldest, richest, and best educated members of the clan had the greatest prestige. They were known as the gentry and were recognized as the clan leaders.

The gentry of each clan in En-p'ing chose representatives to attend meetings in the ancestral hall of one clan where they would all make decisions together concerning the town. A leader, chosen from the strongest clan, presented the questions: where to build a new bridge, how to raise money to heighten the wall around the town, whom to select to guard the crops against field robbers. The representatives discussed each issue until they could agree on what to do and then set about collecting the funds and directing the projects.

The gentry served as intermediaries between their

Clans gave money for schools where boys recited classics.

clan's members and the government officials, known as mandarins, who were sent to En-p'ing by the emperor in Peking. The mandarins were supposed to keep a census, investigate crimes and criminals, and make note of feuds, floods, and famines. They were expected to send reports back to Peking and then do whatever they could to relieve local crises. In actual fact, this once-successful system no longer worked. China was a vast empire with a huge population and inadequate transportation and communication. It was impossible for Peking to control each far-flung village. The mandarins, who took bribes and produced little help from Peking, failed to win the trust of the gentry or of the poor clansmen.

The tax collectors sent from Peking were no more welcome. Every man in En-p'ing who owned land had to pay a tax on it in money or in crops. The landless had to pay a labor tax in money or give day labor—building imperial roads, canals, or bridges, repairing city walls or dikes, or serving in the army. The collectors demanded less than the quota of taxes from the rich in order to keep their friendship and then had to force more money from the poor to fill the coffers bound for Peking. Chinese peasants, sometimes led by scholars who sympathized with their plight, occasionally rioted against the tax collectors. Breaking into government headquarters, they threw expensive furniture, silken cushions, and gauze curtains into heaps and set them afire. But the riots failed; government troops always rushed in and scattered the peasants, flogging any ringleaders they found.

While the clan leaders tried to help their own kin

against the pressures exerted from Peking, they found themselves powerless against the natural forces of over-population and flood. China's millions were concentrated on the coasts and riverbanks. In the crowded Pearl River Delta, there was, on the average, less than a quarter of an acre of cultivable land per person. The annual crop could feed only one third of the population, and the number of people trying to live in the delta kept increasing. The land that had fed one mouth in the 1760's was feeding two in the 1860's. In bad years, peasants ate the bean cakes they normally used as fertilizer, bark, roots, herbs, buds, and seeds, and flour made of ground leaves. Most of them desperately needed more land, but none dared or even wanted to suggest plowing up the sacred graveyards of the ancestors.

In years past, the peasants around En-p'ing had cut the trees on the hillsides for fuel. Now when heavy summer rains fell on the bare hillsides, the water would rush down onto the plains in torrents. Once every few years, furious flood waters would break through the dikes along the river, tearing out rice plants, ripping up trees. Sometimes houses were inundated, furniture swept away, domestic animals drowned, and people killed.

Clan leaders were also powerless to end human violence. Indeed the clans themselves produced violence. Quarrels over land or water rights begun by individuals in towns like En-p'ing developed easily into disputes between their clans. Meeting in their ancestral hall, clan leaders decided whether to challenge their rivals to take the battle to the hills or to fight in the rice paddies where precious crops would be trampled. If one clan decided to attack within the town and managed to force its way into the ancestral hall of its enemy, the invaders smashed ancestral tablets and tore apart genealogical records. In the street outside, clansmen defending their hall fought with clubs, sticks, hoes, and perhaps guns. People were massacred, buildings burned, mud houses demolished, and their contents looted. When government officials arrived to restore order, warring clansmen would flee or hide, determined to take up the fight later.

Some poor peasants left farming and vowed to grow rich by violence. They joined together in clanlike secret societies of roving bandits who kidnaped rich people for ransom and took prisoners to sell to Portuguese and Spanish ship captains. Vessels always lay anchored at the nearby Portuguese town of Macao, ready to carry captives to work at slave wages on the sugar plantations of Cuba or to collect guano from islands off the coast of Peru. In quieter moments, the bandits hid themselves in deserted temples or in peasants' houses. When autumn crops were ripe but not yet harvested, groups of three or four would sneak out into the paddies and fields at night and cut the crops. Law-abiding merchants and farmers were sometimes forced to join these secret societies or pay off the bandits to avoid being robbed. Towns and villages assigned young men to guard the crops against bandits day and night.

Warfare in En-p'ing could erupt from still another source. Most of the people living in the town were called Puntis or natives. But a number of the tenant farmers and some of the shopkeepers and traders were called Hakkas or "stranger people." Although these people had been moving from northern China into the delta and En-p'ing since the 1700's, they were still considered intruders. At first, they had occupied hilly and less fertile districts. But then some Hakkas had tilled land belonging to mandarins and government troops and, through this connection, a number of them were admitted to civil service posts—a kind of social climbing that infuriated the Puntis. When bad floods forced Punti peasants to temporarily abandon their fields outside En-p'ing, Hakkas moved in and occupied them before the Puntis returned. By one means or another, Hakka tenants had gradually acquired more and better land.

Punti peasants remarked unfavorably about the Hakkas, whose customs differed from their own. The Hakkas spoke a different dialect, worshiped a few different gods, and for the most part lived in their own separate villages. Hakka women did not bind their feet, and they were less secluded than Punti women. Hatred grew.

From time to time during the 1850's and 1860's, Hakka tenants of En-p'ing banded together with men of the several Hakka villages nearby and refused to pay the Punti landlords what they thought were exorbitant farm rents. Armed with clubs, sticks, and a few guns, Hakkas slaughtered Punti landlords and set fire to their handsome houses near the center of En-p'ing. Rents would be lowered for a year or two, but eventually the Puntis struck back and killed so many Hakkas that the new settlers gave up their demands and fled from En-p'ing.

Some set up bandit strongholds in the hills, from which they launched guerrilla attacks that added to the frightening way of life in En-p'ing.

Most peasants felt there was nothing they could do about the poverty, famine, floods, and violence that were such a part of their lives:

> All things are prearranged by Fate; for what shall we pray?
> Today knows not the affairs of tomorrow; how shall we plan? . . .
> Good luck comes to all who patiently wait for it: do not be over anxious.
> On this earth are few occasions for laughter; why complain of your lot as a specially hard one? [3]

LEAVING THE ANCESTRAL LANDS

There were some enterprising peasants in the delta who believed that fate had intended a better life. When no amount of hard work would provide their families with enough food and clothing, these peasants sought opportunities elsewhere. Each year after the harvest in En-p'ing, many of them traveled long distances to more prosperous districts to find work and returned home again in time for spring planting. It seemed that the only way for a family to remain together in the ancestral land was for one member to emigrate to a Chinese community overseas and send money back.

Only in 1869 did the Imperial Government relax the law that had made emigration from China punishable by death. Despite the law, men had been bribing officials for decades and leaving the southern coast of China for Malaya, Borneo, Indochina, and the Philippines. There in the *Nan Yang* or Southern Ocean, they lived and worked among kinsfolk who had become successful merchants. The money that they sent home freed their wives from work in the fields, educated their sons, and enabled their families to live more comfortably. Although an emigrant made occasional trips back to his native town or village to beget children, visit aging parents, or perhaps buy a piece of land, he worked in the Nan Yang until he was fifty or sixty. Then he returned home to spend his remaining years with his family, and one of his sons took over his business in the Nan Yang.

Beginning in the 1850's, men in towns like En-p'ing had an alternative to the Nan Yang. Tales of gold in a faraway place called California reached the delta. By the 1860's, educated villagers in En-p'ing were probably reading aloud pamphlets distributed by Chinese travel brokers and American ship captains that advertised:

> Americans [are] a very rich people. They want the [Chinese emigrant] to come and will make him very welcome. There you will have great pay, large houses, and food and clothing of the finest description. . . . Never fear, and you will be lucky. Come to Hong Kong, or to the sign of this house in Canton, and we will instruct you.[4]

During the 1860's, large numbers of peasant farmers left the Pearl River Delta for San Francisco. They did not take their families with them because they had no intention of settling abroad. Some had enough cash hidden in the walls of their houses to pay the forty or fifty dollars that a ticket to San Francisco cost. The rest obtained tickets on credit from a Chinese broker in Hong Kong or from the agent of a California mining or railroad company that was recruiting cheap labor. The emigrant would agree to repay the cost of his passage from his future earnings. Little did he know when he left that it might take months, even years, working for low wages in a mining camp, to settle his debt.

Though optimistic, the emigrant felt some fear as he prepared to leave his family and clan.

> He looks back at the cabin where his mother and his children can still be seen gazing after him, and he wonders how he will feel when, in America, the mornings come and go, with no wife to prepare his meals, no children to hail his coming, no aged parents to give him counsel, and no old neighbors with whom to play at dice, or to gossip away the stolen hours. He looks at the rice fields, notices the ditches he has dug, the furrows which he has so often trod, and the growing weeds that he has so many times destroyed; and he tries to realize at present what his feelings must be when he shall see them no more. . . . He sees before him a hundred graves upon the hillside, among which are those of his ancestors. . . . He believes that unless his body shall at his death lie within the limits of that cemetery, his soul, homeless and foodless, and

> perhaps headless, will wander a beggar and an outcast through the by-ways and slums of an eternal purgatory. He trembles at the thought of a possible burial in a foreign land. [5]

Emigrants left En-p'ing together, each carrying a roll of bedding and his sandals, hat, and food in a basket attached to a carrying-pole. The group cast off in a small sampan before daylight to avoid meeting other townsfolk who might utter unlucky words that would imperil their undertaking. They were carried downstream to the huge mouth of the Pearl River, and a commercial junk, magnificently decorated with dragons, took them on to Hong Kong. Then, in the noisome hold of a ship belonging to the Pacific Mail Steamship Company, they departed for San Francisco.

In time, about half the emigrants returned to China. A few of these would collect their families and sail a second time for San Francisco. Others moved on to the American Middle West and east, settling together in cities. Still others never left California, Oregon, or Idaho where their first jobs had taken them and where they remained, trying to repay the money they had borrowed for passage. They died there and were buried far from the hillside graveyards of their protecting ancestors.

FROM LANDLESSNESS

Millesvik, Sweden, 1880's

A PARISH IN THE PINE FOREST

The farms and manors in the parish of Millesvik were scattered far apart across the countryside on land cleared from the dense pine forest. Avoiding close contact with his neighbors gave the Swedish farmer a feeling of independence. Even poor laborers' huts and fishermen's shanties stood well back from the public road in their own little clearings.

A subdivision of Värmland County, Millesvik Parish spread over part of a fairly flat peninsula that thrust itself into a lake. Although people elsewhere in Sweden were surrounded by mountains, the inhabitants of Millesvik looked out on the deep blue waters of Lake Vänern with its timber rafts, sailboats, fishing craft, and larger ships. Millesvik, however, resembled all the other parishes in Sweden in that its roads and pathways led towards the church, which was the center of the rural community. The building's tall spire was visible from far and near. Close by the church stood the pastor's parsonage and farm, and not far from that, a schoolhouse with the teacher's dwelling and garden, a post office, grocery shop, apothecary's, butcher shop, and general store.

The people of Millesvik Parish seldom missed a Sunday at church, even though some had to walk several miles in harsh weather to attend. Before and after the worship service, they talked in the churchyard with the friends and neighbors whom they seldom saw during the week. From bills tacked on the church door they read of laws passed by the national and local governments, and from the pulpit they heard of births, deaths, and marriages in the parish.

All Swedes were born into the Lutheran Church, which was the state religion, and most of them remained members for the rest of their lives. They were required to attend services weekly, receive communion a certain

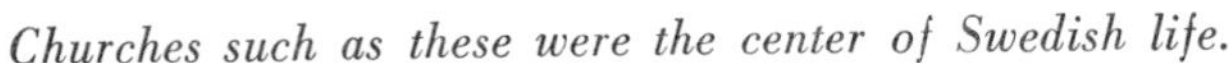

Churches such as these were the center of Swedish life.

number of times during the year, and pay tithes to support the local minister. Although most Swedes went to church willingly, many of them criticized the clergy—who tended to come from the upper class—for being too smug and too distant from their congregations. Parishioners complained that ministers drank too much liquor and frequently neglected their duties, possessed few religious convictions, and gave dull sermons. The parish of Millesvik was probably no exception amidst this general dissatisfaction with the Lutheran Church.

In the distribution of land, too, Millesvik was more or less typical of other rural communities in Sweden. The country people were divided into landowning farmers known as *bönder**, tenant farmers called *torpare,* and farm laborers known as *statare.* A bonde usually owned somewhere between five and fifty acres—the wealthiest a hundred—which he tilled with his family. Here in Värmland County, a bonde usually grew oats on his most fertile land and grazed cattle on the stonier meadows. He grew hay to feed the cattle. The bonde might have as many as seven cows in his barn, a horse in his stable, quite a few sheep, possibly several pigs, and a number of chickens. Large acreage entitled a bonde to nearly the same social rank as the lower gentry. But the gentry, who owned large estates inherited by birth, had priority in government jobs, army offices, and certain church appointments. Poorer bönder, on the other hand, were little better off than the torpare who rented their cabins and up to ten acres of farmland, known as a *torp.*

* *Bönder* is the plural of *bonde.* In pronouncing Swedish names, ä is pronounced like the *a* in *add* and ö is pronounced like the *ea* in *heard.*

A rural road cuts through the flat and timbered land of

southern Sweden in Gustaf Rydberg's "Scanian Landscape."

A typical torpare had only one cow, several sheep and goats, perhaps a horse, a pig, and a few chickens; some had even less. Torpare paid their rent by doing a certain number of days' work for the bonde who owned the land. To add to their incomes, they hired themselves out as farm laborers. If a torpare was able to save enough money from his scanty earnings, he might try to buy a bit of land.

Both bönder and torpare, whom we can collectively call peasants, produced at home almost everything they needed. They raised oats for their bread and grew potatoes, cabbages, and turnips. Their wives milked the cows, churned the butter, pressed the cheese, and sometimes helped in the fields.

Peasants who were well off had plenty of bread, vegetables, eggs, and dairy products to eat. Since they lived near the shores of Lake Vänern, they ate a good deal of fish, and even bought some ocean herring to salt at home. Surplus potatoes were converted into *brännvin,* a kind of whiskey. The poorer rural people, however, ate less well, living on hard rye bread, potatoes, and porridge, with an occasional salt herring. If they had a cow they added milk and cheese to this meager fare.

Often the peasants built their log cabins themselves, finishing them with a thatched or tile roof and a porch. Every cabin, barn, hut, and shanty throughout Sweden was the same rusty color, painted with red ocher to protect the wood against rot. White trim around the casements outlined the windows against the dark red paint on the timber. Pine twigs covered the floors and pine logs burned in the fireplaces. Families lighted their rooms with tallow candles or blazing slips of pitch pine.

Most houses had just one story, though sometimes there was also an attic reached by a stepladder. The main room served as the dining room, sitting room, and often the family bedroom. If grandparents lived in the house, they occupied a smaller bedroom at the back. Adjoining the parlor was a small kitchen, but the housewife did her baking and brewing in separate sheds.

The main room was furnished with a large pine table and occasionally with a writing desk, one or more benches or chairs, and sofas which converted into beds. These were usually hand carved as was the master bed located in an alcove enclosed by curtains. In one corner, a small bookshelf held a leather-bound Bible, a psalm book, and an almanac, as well as a large, loudly ticking clock. The walls of the room might be adorned with pictures of Luther and of Swedish heroes or several blue-and-white-patterned plates. Overhead, a good sup-

A bread pole often held enough bread to last three months.

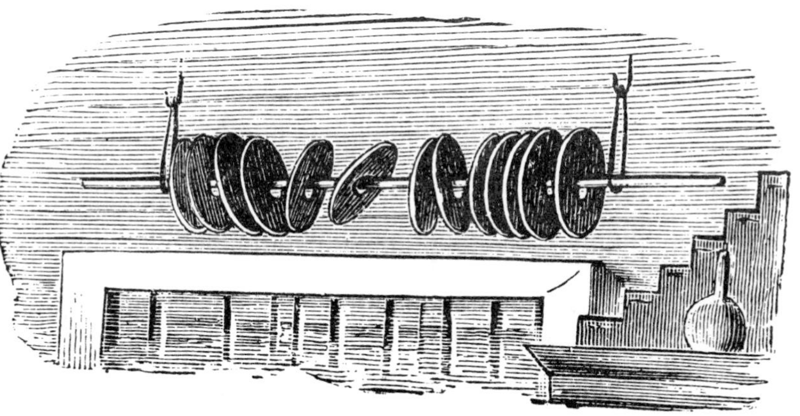

ply of bread, usually thin round discs with holes in the middle, was strung on poles hung from the rafters.

Clothing, like furniture, was made at home. A bonde frequently raised the flax and sheared the wool that his wife spun and wove into clothes for the family, linen for the beds and tables, and colorful hangings for the walls of the house. Some cloth was saved for the visit of the parish tailor who would sew it into the family's best outfits. Everyday clothes were not fancy but kept the peasants warm during the long winter. Most people slept in some of the same clothes they wore for work. Men wore cloth jackets with short leather breeches and wool stockings. When it rained they put on long woolen overcoats. Women tied aprons over their ankle-length skirts

From wool and flax, housewives made clothes like these.

and wore close-fitting jackets over their blouses and kerchiefs over their hair.

Most of the time these peasants wore leather shoes or knee-high boots; they also had wooden shoes which lasted longer, and they sometimes went barefoot in summer. The peasant tanned his own leather from the hides of his cows, oxen, sheep, or pigs. The leather, too, was set aside until the wandering shoemaker came to the farm for several days and made the raw sheets into shoes and boots for the household.

The shoemaker and tailor who visited the family were paid with food, a place to sleep, and a small sum of money. They brought some variety to the otherwise monotonous life on the farm. As they cut and sewed their materials, they told the family what their neighbors were doing, and sometimes they arranged marriages for the peasants' sons and daughters. Other visitors welcomed at the remote farms were the itinerant peddlers. From a peddler, peasants bought weavers' combs, sieves, scissors and knives, clocks, ladders, reed baskets, and iron scythes, none of which they made themselves.

Many families did make things at home to sell in a market town beyond the parish. During the autumn and winter, when the ground was frozen solid or covered with snow, they stood inside at their workbenches or sat by the fire. As fathers and sons built cabinets and carved wood, mothers and daughters knit stockings, caps, and mufflers, wove homespun clothes, and made butter and cheese. Sometimes women gathered in each other's homes to spin, chat, and tell stories.

All boys and girls were required to attend school,

which was free for those whose parents were too poor to pay. The children went to the parish school if they lived near enough; otherwise, an itinerant schoolmaster who wandered from one end of the parish to another, taught them at home. Beginning at five or six, children learned to read, write, and do arithmetic. They memorized Luther's Catechism, studied Bible history, and practiced choral singing. No child could leave school until he had mastered these subjects, usually at age ten. Any child who stayed on until he was fifteen studied geometry, geography, and Swedish history as well. Bright ones, who continued their education at a school in a town beyond the parish, might learn Latin, Greek, French, and German, gymnastics, trigonometry, physics, and other sciences. A few sons of the more prosperous peasants went on to the university at Uppsala or Lund to prepare for the ministry or other professions.

Peasants with seven to twelve children did not have enough work at home for all their sons and daughters who had finished school. So at the age of fifteen, after their confirmation in the Lutheran Church, a few boys were apprenticed to a craftsman and went on to ply their trade around Millesvik or in another parish. Most young people who were sent away from home to work went to one of the gentry or to a neighboring bonde, where they were treated as members of the family. This informal apprenticeship taught them whatever farming skills and household arts they had not learned at home. Work for another peasant usually continued until a young man married, at which point he would try to rent his own plot of land.

All able-bodied youths had to enroll for several years of military service at the age of twenty-one. This did not mean spending all their time in the army, but a certain number of months each year in training. Many young men resented this duty and hated the rigid discipline that haughty upper-class officers enforced. When not away at army camp, these youths generally continued their farming apprenticeships and made their plans for acquiring a wife and a farm—the latter not an easy task for younger sons.

A DECADE OF HARD TIMES

Eventually, most young men went back to work on their fathers' farms until the land was bequeathed to one of the sons, usually the oldest. This Swedish custom of turning over the whole farm to only one son left the others landless. As the population of Sweden increased, the number of sons without land multiplied. In the 1880's, land was so scarce and expensive that those who did not inherit the family farm had little hope of ever acquiring their own.

Often the best that a landless son could do was to rent a cottage and a torp from his father or brother or from some other prosperous man in the parish. The less fortunate found only a couple of acres and could not raise enough food for a family; they had to hire themselves out as part-time farm laborers. During prosperous years they could support themselves, but when crops yielded poorly they could not find work and went hungry.

An increasing number of men found no land, even to rent; they hired themselves out as statare. Some lived like apprentices without contracts in the homes of their employers and received food, clothing, and spending money, but no definite salary. Others, especially married laborers, were hired a year at a time and were housed in one-room cabins with small gardens on their employers' land. Young unmarried women worked as maidservants. Although these young men and women were not always happy with their jobs, the law forbade them to quit; any who did were sought out by the sheriff and forcibly returned to their masters.

Because so many men and women were competing for jobs in Millesvik Parish, wages remained low. Statare and maidservants were the poorest people in that parish as they were everywhere in rural Sweden. Having no land, they had nothing to fall back on when they were out of work and nothing to give them social status in the community.

Social differences were felt among the rural classes. The torpare and statare resented the snobbishness of the bönder, who were arrogant toward their landless neighbors. Even within the rank of the bönder, the size of a man's farm determined his social standing. A bonde with fifty acres would never have considered as a husband for his daughter the son of one with ten acres.

Since status in Sweden depended on the amount of land a person owned, the minister, the gentry, and the government officials, who all lived on large estates in Millesvik, formed the aristocracy of the parish. When members of the aristocracy gave festivals and dances for the local people, they assumed airs of superiority that humiliated the lower classes. Gentry and government officials were given seats of honor at social functions and always sat in the front pews at church. Bönder, torpare, and statare were expected to remove their hats and bow to the gentry when they met on a road or in the churchyard.

The large estates of the gentry, clergy, and government officials assured them political as well as economic and social status. A man had the right to vote only if he owned a lot of land. Throughout Sweden, discontented citizens felt that if they served in the army and paid taxes, they should be allowed to vote.

Although most bönder lacked the political privileges of their rich neighbors, they had been generally well off for years. Millesvik's land was productive and the farming life relatively prosperous. Much depended on the price of grain, which stayed high during the 1850's, 60's, and 70's and brought the bönder substantial profits when they sold their surpluses. The 1880's, however, saw a sharp drop in the price of grain, which brought a severe depression.

The trouble stemmed from the recent cultivation of virgin land in Russia, Australia, Argentina, Canada, and the United States. The invention of the harvester and the binder (first used in the United States in 1872 and 1880, respectively) made it possible to farm these large areas with little hand labor. At the same time, competition among the growing number of railroad companies and steamship lines reduced freight rates. With low rates, the large harvests of grain from the sparsely populated lands could be shipped great distances cheaply and sold in the heavily populated areas of the world, including northern and western Europe. American grain was sold in the towns and parishes of Sweden for less money than the local grain. As a result, the price of Swedish grain kept dropping to meet the low prices of the imported grain. In the 1880's, grain prices were at their lowest in fifty years. The profits of the Swedish bönder decreased accordingly; some peasants went bankrupt.

At the same time that this depression was creating hardship for the landholding bönder of Millesvik, a decline in winter work was making life more difficult than ever for the poorer landless people of the parish. Many of them had traveled every winter to Norrland (the northern provinces) to work for pay in the forests, leaving their families at home. For decades the timber corporations had depended on the labor of these traveling workers from Värmland since so few people lived in Norrland in the early part of the century. They had built railroads, cut trees, floated and hauled timber, or worked at machines in the north's new paper and sawmills, where they earned over three times as much as in ordinary farm work. By the 1880's, however, so many people had settled permanently in Norrland that winter workers from Värmland were no longer needed.

Meanwhile, the lumber companies were beginning to cut trees south of Norrland and to buy up tracts of land in Värmland itself. Whenever a farm was up for sale in Millesvik it was sold to the highest bidder. That person was often not a local farmer or a landless son wanting to marry but the representative of a lumber company. Once the sale was completed, farming stopped

Statare at work for a timber company during the winter.

and the fields were planted with pines. In a county where tillable land was already in short supply, the planting of trees on field after field increased the sense of frustration among farmers struggling to buy new land or just to hold on to the old.

With little or no land, low grain prices, no jobs in winter, and the encroachment of lumber companies, more and more bönder, torpare, and statare looked for alternatives to staying home and growing poorer. Some moved to the newly industrialized cities of Sweden, but America appealed to those who wanted their own farms.

AMERICA FEVER

Over the last forty years, a number of Swedes had emigrated to the United States. Many of them came from the three percent of the people who belonged to sects other than the Lutheran Church. Dissenters had been threatened with fines and imprisonment as late as 1873.

Even after they became legally free to worship as they pleased, they often felt socially ostracized, and they were passed over in government jobs. Many preferred to move to a country where religious beliefs made no difference. The Baptist, Mormon, and Methodist sects had been introduced into Sweden through American influence, and their members had an open invitation to join the mother churches in America.

In the 1860's, distressing crop failures sent a large number of Lutheran peasants across the Atlantic. By the 1880's, nearly every household in rural Sweden knew someone who had settled in America. When a man who had been living there came back to visit his family, he would brag about how well he was living, showing off a gold watch as a symbol of his new wealth. He might be wearing expensive clothes and carrying enough American money to treat his friends to brännvin while he exclaimed over America's high wages and cheap food. Invariably, when these visitors returned to the United States, they took along a number of friends and relatives.

During the 1880's, "America fever" swept over the parish of Millesvik as letters from America reached almost every home. For farmers accustomed to seeking seasonal work in Norrland, it seemed natural to go to America when they could no longer find winter jobs in their own provinces. In the United States, farm laborers and maidservants were in great demand.

So many people left Millesvik Parish that its population in 1909 was only half of what it had been in 1865. More went during the 1880's than in any other decade. The largest number of these emigrants hoped to find higher wages or land to buy. A few left for personal reasons: a man who had served a jail sentence for a small crime hoped to make a fresh start; a daughter left to escape marrying the young man her parents had selected. Some were simply caught up in the excitement of emigration.

Publicity about America heightened the excitement. Swedish newspapers contained many advertisements placed by steamship companies offering cheap passage across the Atlantic and by railroad and land companies in the United States encouraging laborers and settlers. Swedes eagerly read guidebooks written for emigrants, which described in detail the climate, geography, job opportunities, wages, and cost of land in Minnesota, Wisconsin, the Dakotas, Kansas, Nebraska, and other states. These books told them what to take, urged them to learn some English before leaving, and warned them not to fall into the hands of swindlers on the way. Whenever Swedes decided to leave their country, local representatives of emigrant companies would plan their routes and sell them tickets to any place in the United States.

Those who did not trust the words printed in newspapers and books were lured to America by assurances from relatives and friends whose letters guaranteed abundance:

> We have good bread and wheat flour and as much beef and pork as we desire for each meal. We have all the butter, eggs, and milk we need.[1]

More important to the peasants than plenty of food were the millions of acres of cheap virgin land described in advertisements, guidebooks, and letters. The United States Government promised to give 160 acres to any adult who would farm them. Naturally, tracts this size seemed incredible to bönder who had small farms in Sweden and to young men who would never have land of their own. The fact that a friend, formerly a humble torpare, was now the owner of a 160-acre farm in Minnesota or Illinois made the farms in Sweden seem smaller than ever. Letters from America reported that men and women could earn nearly three times as much in a day as at home and that "day laborers are able to save money here—an impossibility in Sweden." The letter writer continued, "I know of many who own farms who didn't even have gruel in Sweden." [2]

Swedes learned that a settler in America would pay hardly any taxes until he became a landowner, and even then taxes were low. In Sweden, on the other hand, all bönder paid high land taxes and torpare paid them indirectly in the form of higher rents. Everyone, including statare, had to pay income taxes, something no American would be required to do until 1913.

Men and women came to understand that success in America depended not on birth and inheritance but on plain hard work. Immigrants who were industrious could be almost certain of becoming landowners with horses and wagons and acres of fields within a few years. Meanwhile, no one would look down on a farm laborer in America, since

> a farmer who owned a thousand acres of farmland worked himself all day with his hired men . . . In

America hired men and maids could leave their service when they wanted without punishment. [3]

Letters convinced torpare and statare that they would find social equality as well as opportunity in America. They would be called "mister" and would be required to call no one "sir." They could even greet others without having to remove their hats! The more that humble Swedes heard about the political system in America, the more it appealed to them. There were no kings and no gentry. Every man was eligible to vote as soon as he became a citizen, and a poor man's vote counted as much as a millionaire's. To young men who faced military training, prospects in America seemed especially inviting, because the United States had no service requirement in the 1880's. Many youths who intended to leave eventually for economic reasons decided to leave before they reached twenty-one to escape being drafted.

Though most letters from America spoke of opportunities, an occasional one mentioned droughts, hailstorms, blizzards, or plagues of grasshoppers and locusts. Even so, the letter-writers rarely sounded discouraged. The most exciting letters were those that contained prepaid tickets to America and promised a job upon arrival. Statare and maidservants with no land of their own would have found it difficult to emigrate without such help, since a ticket cost the equivalent of several years' wages.

Young men and women by the score left Millesvik and other districts of southern and central Sweden in the 1880's. They departed in groups, joining families of bönder who had sold their farms to lumber companies and to other individuals from their parish. Emigrants loaded flat horsedrawn carts with chests, boxes, sacks, baskets, and bundles. At the home gate, they bade farewell to those of the family who stayed behind. They would write from America, of course, perhaps even send money back so others could follow; but the intervals between the letters would grow longer.

Some drove their horses the twelve miles north to Säffle where they would catch a train to Göteborg on the coast. Others would take a boat across Lake Vänern and along the Göta Kanal to Göteborg. Then a steamer would carry them, crowded into steerage, the forty-five hundred miles to New York. In Manhattan, the immigrants would board a train to Albany and on to Buffalo and Chicago. Some might stay in Chicago, but most would seek out the familiar flat and lake-filled landscape of the prairie states in the upper Mississippi Valley or farther west. Here they would build their log cabins and barns far apart from those of their neighbors and till more land than their fathers in Sweden had ever hoped to own.

FROM FUTILITY

Bisacquino, Sicily, 1900-1910

THE GRIMNESS OF NATURE

The piazza or main square at the center of Bisacquino teemed with noisy people. This was where the town crier began his daily tour of the town, announcing the price of fish and the dreaded dates when rents and taxes must be paid. Here women sold vegetables to other women who bargained loudly for a good price. Street vendors passed through hawking their fruits and vegetables, eggs, octopuses, and roasted nuts, charcoal, needles, thread, and candles. The wares that did not fit into hand baskets were loaded onto brightly painted two-wheeled carts drawn by scrawny donkeys: "Melons! Melons! I've got nice juicy melons! Taste how sweet!" Working men gathered around the fountain in the piazza on Sundays to relax and talk. And during the week, men without jobs lounged there in company with cripples on crutches who begged for alms at the center of town.

The immense Roman Catholic church that opened onto the piazza of Bisacquino looked magnificent in con-

This mountain town near Palermo resembled Bisacquino with

trast to its dingy surroundings in this mountain town of western Sicily. Narrow streets radiated outward from the center of town, some unpaved and dusty, others laid over with cobblestones; those running up or down slopes were built as flights of steps. The dilapidated one-story houses that stood close together on both sides of the narrow streets were built of a gray stone that blended into the surrounding landscape. Some of these houses had vegetable gardens, and a few olive trees, but others had no open spaces at all around them.

its gray stone houses, towering spires, and narrow streets.

About eight thousand people lived in Bisacquino in the early 1900's. Most of them were *contadini** (peasants), who owned no land but worked in fields that belonged to someone else. Like contadini all over Sicily and southern Italy, they lived in isolation from the outside world. They spoke a dialect different from those of people in other parts of Italy, even in other parts of the

* Most singular Italian nouns end in *o* or *a*. They form their plurals by changing the *o* ending to *i* or the *a* ending to *e*. Thus *contadini* is the plural of *contadino*, *feste* is the plural of *festa* (festival).

island of Sicily. Some had never ventured beyond the next village, four miles away. For them, Italy was Bisacquino. Their word for a town or region was *paese* and for their fellow inhabitants *paesani.* All outsiders were regarded with suspicion.

Nothing ever seemed to change in Bisacquino. Its people knew no other way of life than the one that their ancestors had led for centuries. Like their ancestors before them, they were always worriedly expecting earthquakes, drought, malaria, and erosion.

Earthquakes attacked suddenly and without warning perhaps once in a decade somewhere in Sicily. They destroyed crops, houses, and people. Fear of them made the people of Bisacquino feel helpless and uncertain of the future. No one wanted to risk spending his savings on farm buildings, machines, or animals, only to have an earthquake destroy them.

Drought, though more predictable than earthquakes, created almost as many problems. The contadini knew that during six or seven months of the year the grass would turn brown from the drought and the riverbeds would dry to mud or cracked earth. There was so little rain during the summer that even the richest soil of the region would not produce much, and the soil of Bisacquino was rocky and unfertile. The only plants that could survive such a long dry season were olives and figs, wheat and grapes, and these were the mainstays of the Sicilian diet. A man could raise fruits and vegetables to vary his diet only if he could irrigate them from a spring, but land with a spring was expensive to rent. When an occasional wetter season brought more abundant crops, contadino families were happy because they had more to eat.

Lack of rainfall limited not only the crops but also the animals that the contadini could raise. A few sheep and goats could endure the yearly drought by grazing the parched hillsides, but cows and horses needed more water and grass. Oxen and mules could survive, and they were used to do the heavy work of farming.

Heavy rains that fell during the cooler months were no help but only collected in troublesome pools and created another hazard. Stagnant pools became breeding places for mosquitoes, the spreaders of malaria. Once contracted, malaria could last a lifetime. It kept men away from the fields for long stretches and returned them to work in weak condition. Many of the people of Bisacquino looked thin, pale, and often yellow from malaria.

Cows did climb the streets of rainier towns than Bisacquino.

To avoid the mosquitoes, which bit at night, the contadini had to live in the hills, away from the low-lying land where the stagnant pools collected and where they farmed. They wasted much of their energy walking down the steep, stony hillsides to the fields at dawn and home again in the evening. Those who escaped malaria probably suffered from typhoid, rheumatic fever, smallpox, or intestinal ailments. Many people went through life without ever feeling well, and a man of thirty might look fifty-five.

Another scourge of nature against which the people of Bisacquino felt powerless was erosion. Sicily had once been heavily wooded and fertile. But through the years, men had cut down trees to clear more farm land, and eventually the fertile topsoil washed off the hillsides and blocked the streams. The slowed streams began to meander and to form lakes, spreading sand and gravel over once good land that gradually had to be abandoned. People did not replant any trees because they needed every bit of land that had been cleared. Even those who realized that deforestation caused erosion would not replant because their forefathers had never done so.

BOUND BY TRADITION

Like poor peasants in isolated towns all over the world, the paesani of Bisacquino found security by following the ways of their ancestors. They assumed that any change would be useless and might make matters worse. Besides, combating the forces of nature with irrigation projects, health care, and reforestation would have taken education, money, and community cooperation, and the contadini had none of these.

Four out of five inhabitants could neither read nor count beyond fifty. Parents considered it more important for their children to help weed fields and remove stones than to go to school. The small, dirty, and poorly attended schools of communities like Bisacquino did not attract pupils anyway and did not appear to the contadini to be places where anything of importance could be learned.

Money that the contadini might have spent on medicine, farm buildings, or better land had to be paid in taxes to the thirty-year-old government in Rome, capital of the new nation of Italy. The contadini paid taxes on their houses and furniture, and on salt, tobacco, sugar, and liquor. The government spent much of Bisacquino's tax revenue on extravagant monuments, theaters, and festivals for the large cities of Italy and on supporting an army and navy; almost none went back to the small towns.

Even the proprietors who owned most of the land around Bisacquino did nothing to help the contadini. They knew that they could maintain their own higher standard of living only by keeping the contadini poor. Many of them were constantly in debt themselves from heavy land taxes, and few could have afforded good plows or better fertilizers if they had wanted their tenants to have them. Actually, they did not seem to care what happened on their land so long as they received their rents. Most of them did not live in Bisacquino and seldom even visited their estates because they preferred the gayer life of Palermo, the largest city in Sicily.

Among the contadini themselves, there was no community cooperation. The family was the group to which men felt loyalty. Parents loved children and usually had at least four of them. It was expected that everyone would think of his family first. A son, for example, might have to end his training as a shoemaker in order to earn money for his sister's dowry. A father, playing cards and chatting with a small group of men, would never suggest a community irrigation project that would take time and money away from supporting his family. With little land and the constant threat of natural catastrophe, parents devoted themselves to protecting their children from starvation, death, and evil ways so that they, too, might grow up and marry and bear children.

Family loyalty even endangered the lives of fellow paesani, since a man sometimes attempted to settle his own or his family's quarrels by killing his adversary. This disastrous ancient custom, known as the vendetta, was responsible for many murders. Families living in hatred and suspicion of each other added to the hostility of the environment.

Paesani hesitated to undertake any new kind of responsibility in the community just as they avoided change in any aspect of their daily activities. This adherence to tradition was revealed over and over again in the lives of the *mezzadri* and *giornalieri*, the two categories of contadini. Mezzadri were tenant farmers who paid the proprietors with half (*mezzo* means half) of the crops they raised. The poorer giornalieri, who could not even afford to rent, had to hire themselves out as day (*giorno* means day) or seasonal laborers.

Even if he could have afforded it, the average mezzadro would not have bought farm equipment, since he regarded machines as an attempt "to go ahead of the Eternal Father, who therefore punishes him with bad harvests."[1] Instead, many mezzadri used an ancient Roman type of plow which simply scratched the soil. Some did not even use that, but stayed with the primitive hand hoe called a *zappa.* It took weeks to prepare a single field of wheat with a zappa. Many would not fertilize with manure because they believed that it dirtied the land. They sowed the seed by hand and used a hand sickle to reap. Oxen or mules threshed the wheat by tramping on the floor where it lay, and men separated the chaff from the grain by throwing the stalks up into the wind. Mules operated the presses that made olive oil. And men stamped on grapes to squeeze out the juice used to make wine. Such farming had been seen near Bisacquino two thousand years earlier in the days of the Roman Empire.

A mezzadro grew mostly wheat, though he might have a few olive and fig trees. He planted one crop of wheat a year, and if that failed, he sat back and did no more, convinced that his battle against nature was futile. The mezzadro believed that only luck or the favor of the saints brought him success, not hard work, though he did plenty of that.

A mezzadro's day began as he and his sons arose in the dark, around four in the morning, to do as much work as they could before the sun got hot. They walked the four or five miles to their fields, carrying heavy hoes over their shoulders and leading a donkey or mule laden with other tools down the rocky mountain footpath. After working a few hours, they breakfasted on stale dark bread and a few figs and tomatoes, or perhaps olives and a bit of fish that they had carried to the fields wrapped in a napkin. Then they resumed their work. More of the same food was served for lunch at noon. Mezzadri returned to Bisacquino after sunset, in small groups, walking behind their donkeys. No one used a cart because a cart could not keep to the trails down the steep hillsides.

There was very little work during the year for the

Guided by contadini, mules pull plows over the stony soil of open fields that stretch below one of Sicily's hill towns.

poorer day laborers. Throughout the summer months, these giornalieri, who made up more than half the population of Bisacquino, assembled at dawn in the piazza. Each carried a scythe over his shoulder and wore a red handkerchief tied around his head. Much as slaves at a slave market, they waited to be chosen for work.

Proprietors, overseers, and mezzadri came to pick out the strongest four or five laborers they could find. Men who were not hired spent the day gossiping or playing cards in the piazza or in local cafés. But all despaired if they failed to get work because they would not be able to feed their families.

Reaping during June and July from sunrise to sunset

provided the giornalieri with their only regular work of the year. During May, they might hoe, and after the wheat harvest, they might thresh and glean. In autumn, they picked grapes and olives. At other times of the year, a giornaliero might hunt snails or gather fennel and wild chicory to sell. In winter, he sometimes cleaned out stables or went to the mountains to collect *disa,* a tough grass used to make brooms and stuffed mattresses. Giornalieri seldom earned wages on more than 120 days of the year. Since they had no savings, they lived on the edge of starvation on the other 245 days.

There were no mines or factories to provide jobs for people who could not find work in the fields. But Bisacquino was more fortunate than many communities because there were stone quarries nearby where some men and a few women earned money squaring stones for road pavements. Even children ten and twelve years old labored from six in the morning until six at night, with only an hour's break for food at midday, carrying stones to the crushing mill.

Poverty, hunger, lack of work, and worry about the future brought on *la miseria,* the state of melancholy that accounted for the sad expressions on the faces of many of the contadini, both mezzadri and giornalieri. The contadini dreaded any ill fortune, sickness, or accident. Such disasters would force the mezzadro to sell the bit of land he had saved for years to buy.

Often it seemed to the contadino that there was no hope, for no matter how hard he worked he could never do better. Because work on the land was considered

Four reapers with scythes stand in a field of ripe wheat.

degrading in Bisacquino, proprietors, professionals, merchants, office workers, and craftsmen refused to let their daughters marry the sons of the contadini. A contadino could not afford to apprentice his son to a craftsman. He knew his children's lives would be no better than his, the future no better than the past.

CONTADINI AT HOME

Almost no one in Bisacquino earned enough money to live comfortably. Only the few proprietors who stayed in town and the prosperous shopkeepers could afford the two-story houses with balconies overlooking the main streets. Mezzadri and giornalieri lived away from the center of town. Around their houses and in the streets, pigs grubbed in piles of garbage and flies bred in manure and refuse heaps.

The houses were so small and dark that the contadini

spent most of their time out of doors. The street was the parlor. Children romped there. Men met to bowl, play cards, gamble, or joke and talk with each other. During warm weather, the men often slept in the street. Women carried chairs outside and sat together in the sun, sewing, embroidering, or knitting. They made blankets and bedspreads and most of the clothes for their families. As they worked they sometimes sang. Women combed their hair outdoors. Often, they cooked over outdoor fires or baked their long or round loaves of bread in a stone oven in the corner of the yard.

It was easy to see why the contadini chose not to spend any more time than they had to inside their houses:

> One room . . . served as a kitchen, bedroom, and usually as quarters for the barnyard animals as well. . . . On one side of the room was the stove; . . . and the walls and ceiling were blackened with smoke. The only light was that from the door. The room was almost entirely filled by an enormous bed, much larger than an ordinary double bed; in it slept the whole family, father, mother, and children. [2]

By rolling back the mattress of the bed in the daytime, the housewife could use the boards underneath as a table or as a counter for making bread.

Red peppers and bunches of garlic were set in rows above the fireplace, which was the only source of heat in most houses. Strings of onions, dried mushrooms, tomatoes, melons, and salami hung from the rafters. Sausages were stored in brine and grain in a coffin-like box.

At eight or nine in the evening, a family finally sat down together to a meal. It was dark by then, and only on special occasions was the table brightened by the light of a wick floating in a clay bowl filled with oil. The meal began with thick bean soup and bread; salad and green vegetables were served in season. The main dish might consist of potatoes, homemade spaghetti with tomato sauce and grated cheese, or a mush made of boiled beans thickened with cornmeal. Occasionally, the family had fish, and on Sundays the spaghetti was often served with meat sauce. The hog, if the family had one, was slaughtered in December, and the salami and sausages usually lasted until June or July. Fresh or dried fruit ended the meal. Contadini sometimes drank wine mixed with water or *caffè*, a hot drink made from roasted and ground grain. Real coffee cost too much. In slow months, giornalieri often had little more to eat than dry bread soaked in olive oil and salt.

Women and girls kept busy with domestic chores. Since their houses had neither toilets nor water taps, they walked to one of the fountains in the town for water, carrying tall earthenware or copper pitchers on their heads. Dust blew into the house constantly from the dry dirt road, so on Saturdays every housewife swept her floor, scalded all utensils, scrubbed the table, and polished the copperware.

Washday came once every three or four weeks. Some women did their washing in the large tanks of the nearest fountain. Others carried bundles of washing on their heads to a stream. They knelt at the edge and spent the whole day tirelessly rubbing the dirty clothes against a

Two girls carry jugs of water home from the town fountain.

rock or a washboard, rinsing them in the river, spreading them out to dry, and gossiping with other women.

From sheep's wool, contadini women spun, wove, and sewed most of the clothes for their families. Many Sicilian men wore long, colored caps with tassels falling to the shoulders or sometimes to the knees. Men pulled each other's tassels as a greeting. Women's dresses were usually black, since deaths in the family were frequent, and the women had to wear mourning for ten years. A woman added a black cloth shawl, known as a *mantillina*, over her head and shoulders to hide herself from the eyes of men whenever she went outdoors.

Young girls and boys were kept strictly apart at school, at work, and at play. By age six or seven, when girls could handle the necessary tools, they were no longer supposed to play games but to busy themselves learning to spin, weave, and sew. An unmarried girl had to avoid looking at men, and when working near her house she sat with her back to the street. When she was fifteen or so, her parents arranged for her to marry one of the young men of the town. As a married woman, she was not supposed to look at any man but her own husband. This seclusion of women was one of the ancient customs still practiced in Sicily in the early 1900's, and almost no one questioned it.

PLEASING GOD AND THE SAINTS

The people of Bisacquino, like people throughout Italy, were Roman Catholics. Yet children received little religious instruction, and many men went to church only on Easter and other religious holidays, or for baptisms, weddings, and funerals. Women, on the other hand, went to church every evening of the year as well as to mass on Sundays.

The daily lives of these people were full of religious rituals that attempted to please God so that He would bring them good fortune. Most families said grace, and the children kissed the bread in thanksgiving to God for their food. They crossed themselves as a blessing to ward off evil and said a prayer before starting any work, whether reaping in the fields or baking bread at home. Before harvesting the grain every summer, the contadini followed a priest, dressed in his vestments, to the top of a hill overlooking the ripening fields of wheat. An acolyte swung an incense burner. The priest raised his arm to bless the surrounding countryside, asking for God's beneficent presence during the harvest season. Although a Catholic priest conducted this ceremony, it was reminiscent of Roman times when farmers offered sacrifices to their gods for a good harvest.

Contadini carried charms to ward off the "evil eye," a power present in certain men and women who could, by a quick glance, cause loss of crops, molding of foodstuffs, injury, disease, or death. Contadini believed that magic, usually some incantation, could cure almost any illness. The dead were carefully respected with proper funerals and the wearing of black for a long time.

Although Sicilians were considered Christians, their religion did not center around Christianity's paternal God. They thought of God as a Being who brought them little but hardship, and they did not know how to satisfy Him. Many people in Bisacquino believed that certain saints were more approachable than God and more willing to grant them the protection they needed. Therefore, they prayed frequently to these saints and lighted candles in the church before their statues, rather than at the main altar. The clothes of a sick person would be laid at the feet of a statue in the belief that the saint's power would make the sick person well as soon as he put the clothes back on. Worshiping saints was a more ancient religion than Christianity. These saints had been Christians whom the Church had officially recognized for their charitable deeds; but they played the same part in the life of Bisacquino as had the gods and spirits of the Greeks and Romans.

The people of Bisacquino eagerly anticipated the summer religious festivals, known as *feste,* during which they showed their devotion to various saints. The most important festa was that held in honor of the patron saint of their town. All but the most essential work stopped. The day began with paesani praising the saint by attending mass. Special tapers were lighted, and paper decorations, draperies, and flags festooned the church both inside and out. A statue of the patron saint was carried through the streets to the accompaniment of a brass band. A procession of men and boys in festive clothes followed the band and threw flowers at the statue while women in the more prosperous streets of town watched from their balconies, over which they had hung brightly colored bedspreads and banners.

Only the midday meal took people off the streets on festa days. Each housewife brought out her best cutlery, a white tablecloth, and embroidered napkins. The poorest families ate some kind of meat, even if just a scrap. Youths began the afternoon festivities with target shooting and betting. A fortune teller dressed in weird clothes wandered among the crowd. Comedians, magicians, jugglers, or a couple of prize fighters performed. The shouts of auctioneers and nougat peddlers filled the air. Horse races were held in the streets as everyone watched, and some placed bets. On the evening of a festa, fireworks were set off. They were intended to make a noise that would be heard in heaven by the patron saint as he watched and enjoyed the day passed in his name.

AN END TO ISOLATION

In the north of Italy, where the environment was less harsh and the people had a sea-going tradition, men had been searching for years for higher wages and better opportunities. Northern Italians would travel to other districts or to other European countries in search of temporary work after their own harvest each year. In southern Italy and Sicily, on the other hand, men had been forbidden to emigrate until early in the 1800's. Italy's north and south had become united in 1870, and from that point on, communication between the various Italian states began to improve, and ideas current in the north spread southward. During the late 1800's, the notion that there was work to be had elsewhere finally reached Sicily, the most southern and remote of the Italian states.

As more and more people were born in Bisacquino, it became less possible for them to maintain even the marginal existence of their ancestors. If men could not earn their bread in their own paese they had to get out. At first, only the most ambitious took a chance, left Bisacquino, and looked for work elsewhere. These men usually found jobs in Palermo, where they heard talk of other employment farther away. Soon more men wanted to leave the small towns and go wherever they thought opportunities would be good and wages high. Some followed their friends to Palermo, and others journeyed to the mainland of Italy. Some crossed the Mediterranean to work for a season or two in North Africa, and some crossed the Atlantic to South and North America.

The attraction of the United States was strong, for unskilled workers were urgently needed there to help build railroads, subways, tunnels, waterworks, and skyscrapers. Word reached Sicily that jobs awaited all who came. From steamship companies eager to sell tickets to potential passengers, the paesani heard about good working conditions and high wages in America.

The first few Italians who struck out for New York

found jobs quickly and their letters persuaded others to follow. From time to time, men who had been to America returned to their paese, boasting of success. They wore new clothes, and some showed off gold and silver fillings in their teeth. They had acquired more education and new skills. Tales of high wages to be earned in America spread rapidly around a small town like Bisacquino and encouraged others to go there.

In isolated villages and towns all over Sicily, increasing numbers of mezzadri and craftsmen who were eager to earn more money decided to leave. Many mezzadri had grown too poor to afford new clothes and shoes or repairs for their houses and tools, with the result that the craftsmen who made these things had become poorer also. They sold carts, animals, pieces of furniture, and perhaps even a bit of land to raise money for passage. Proprietors left, too, because they felt oppressed by heavy taxes and poor harvests.

It was not proprietors, mezzadri, and craftsmen, however, who set out for America from Sicily and southern Italy in the greatest numbers; it was the miserable giornalieri. Unlike peasants in other countries, they felt few sentimental ties to the soil or to their work on it, and they had recently begun to move around for jobs. The newly unified state of Italy did not exert any patriotic pull: "Italy is for us whoever gives us our bread." [3] Their loyalty remained with their families, with some additional sentiment reserved for their paese.

Carrying small bundles of clothing and food, craftsmen, mezzadri, and giornalieri left their paese and walked or rode their donkeys up and down hills to the nearest railroad station. Some emigrants from Bisacquino wearily trudged the fifty miles to Palermo on the coast.

There the tall buildings and the streets crowded with noisy coaches bewildered some of the paesani. They struggled to locate the ticket agent and to find a place to stay until their ship departed. They watched their precious savings dwindle, guarded against pickpockets, and fought the temptation to gamble with what was left. The strange confusion of Palermo, so near home and yet so different from Bisacquino in the hills, was a forewarning of what immensity and foreignness they would meet in New York City when they reached the other shore.

Despite their yearning to leave, the ticket from Palermo to New York City cost thirty dollars, more than men who earned sixty dollars a year could hope to save. A relative or friend who had gone before might send a ticket enclosed in a letter:

> Come to America and I will take care of you, give you work, and I will assist you in any way that I can. [4]

But if there was no willing relative in America, a giornaliero who was determined to go there could join the company of a padrone.

A padrone was a labor boss who obtained tickets and jobs for giornalieri going to America. Originally a contadino himself, the padrone acted as an intermediary between the simple paesani from towns like Bisacquino, and demanding employers in one of the most advanced industrial nations of the world. But he drained the giornalieri of almost every penny that they earned in America. The giornalieri had emigrated alone, intending to save money and return to their paese when they could afford land for themselves, dowries for their daughters, and apprentice fees for their sons. As it turned out, it usually took years of repaying the padrone before a giornaliero could begin to save for his family.

An increasing number of emigrants did not go back to Italy to live. They spent their savings on steamship tickets to bring their families to America. Between 1900 and 1910, nearly two million people left Sicily and southern Italy for the United States. They settled first in cities along the northeastern seaboard, and later some went into the Middle West and to the Gulf and Pacific coasts. Surrounded by people of many national backgrounds whose ties to their homelands were strong, paesani began to feel patriotism for Italy, but it was the more personal ties to their families and their paese that drew them back, late in life, to visit isolated towns like Bisacquino.

FROM OPPRESSION

Polotsk, Russia, 1900-1914

THE SHTETL

Huddled together in crowded towns, the Jews of Russia barely kept from starving, and they lived in constant fear of murderous persecutions known as pogroms. They were comforted by remembering that their wandering people had endured ill fortune throughout much of their history, and they were strengthened by thinking that God was testing them with more.

Studying the Torah, the first five books of the Bible, and the Talmud, the voluminous interpretations of the Torah and its laws, and celebrating the Sabbath and other Jewish festivals brought some happiness into their uneasy lives. No matter how heavy the oppression, Jews lived by the maxim "It is hard to be a Jew and it is good to be a Jew." [1]

The Jews called Polotsk a *shtetl* (town in Yiddish*)

* Yiddish, the language that the Jews spoke, was a German dialect that originated among Jews in the upper and middle Rhine basin around the year 1000. When certain Jews fled persecution in this region in later years, they took their language with them to eastern Europe. Yiddish combines elements of medieval German and Hebrew, and also contains some Old French and Slavonic words.

and greeted fellow Jews with *sholem aleichem*, "peace to you," when they met along its streets. They tended to live on certain streets of the shtetl where their small synagogues were interspersed with shabby, one-story shops and houses. In most of these houses, one room served as workshop, kitchen, laundry, living room, study, and sleeping quarters. A family felt fortunate to have a vegetable garden enclosed by a tumble-down fence. Chickens and geese, a few goats, and an occasional cow shared the streets, the yards, and sometimes the houses. The two-story houses of the few dozen rich Jews in Polotsk stood around its market place, a large paved square at one end of town with a public well. The narrow streets led away from there to the Dvina and Polota Rivers, past gentile (non-Jewish) houses, and outward to fields and woods. These streets were the only world known to many of the residents.

The eleven thousand Jews of Polotsk, over half the population of the town, had no political rights and no civil liberties, and they were prevented from earning an adequate livelihood. Forbidden to live in the villages of the countryside, they could neither farm nor work in the mines or forests or in any of the factories located outside the towns or cities. Few Jews were admitted to Russian universities and technical schools, and without a Russian education, they could not dream of professional careers. They were barred from all government jobs and from teaching posts in Russian high schools and universities, and they could not become officers in the army.

The Jews of Polotsk, along with most of the five

Jewish life, and death, were confined to shtetl streets.

million Jews in Russia, were obliged to stay within the provinces along Russia's western border, a district which came to be called the Pale of Permanent Jewish Settlement. The Russian government did not consider the Jews to be Russians, but outsiders, and they wanted to keep them from competing for their livelihoods with Russia's Slavic and Christian population. If Jews could live in the country they might take some land away from Russian peasants, and if they could settle in all towns and cities they might take profits away from Russian businessmen throughout the empire.

Within the Pale, small-scale commerce and handicrafts were just about the only occupations open to the Jews. As a result, almost all of the butchers and bakers, plumbers, carpenters, and blacksmiths of Polotsk were Jewish. There were innumerable tailors and shoemakers among the men, dressmakers and milliners among the women. Other Jews were book peddlers and jewelers, innkeepers, dealers in agricultural produce, and sellers of household goods, dry goods, and clothing. Polotsk probably had ten times as many craftsmen and stores as were needed. Its Jewish artisans and shopkeepers competed bitterly for the business of other Jews and of gentiles in town and of the peasants on the outskirts, who were all gentiles.

Among the Jews, daily life and religion could not be separated, since Judaism was a way of life. Each generation learned to pray and work, eat and dress, study and marry as its fathers had for centuries, according to the Law set forth in the Torah and elaborated by the Talmudic writings. A good Jew said his prayers three times a day. During his morning prayers, he wore his prayer shawl over his head, and every day except the Sabbath he bound his phylacteries (two small leather boxes containing strips of parchment on which certain of God's Commandments were written) to his left arm and his forehead, for the Bible said, "Thou shalt bind them for a sign upon thine hand, and they shall be as frontlets between thine eyes."

Jewish men and boys kept their heads covered at all times with a hat or with a *yarmulke* (skullcap) in reverence to God. They also wore a ritual undergarment with knotted fringes showing beneath their shirts or jackets. Through Moses, God had instructed the people of Israel to "make . . . fringes in the borders of their garments . . . that ye may look upon it and remember all the commandments of the Lord." The caftan, a long black gabardine overcoat, was the usual attire for men. Many men wore earlocks and almost all had beards, since neither should be cut by scissors or a blade. Their wives wore kerchiefs or wigs over closely cropped hair, a custom intended to keep them from looking too attractive after marriage.

The food that Jewish housewives prepared was always kosher, that is, prepared according to the dietary laws set down in the Scriptures. Animals and chickens had to be slaughtered in a prescribed way and certain foods, such as pork and shellfish, were forbidden. Dairy foods could not be mixed with meat or poultry, nor eaten at the same meal, in obedience to the Biblical injunction: "Thou shalt not seethe the kid in the milk of its mother." There were, however, plenty of neutral foods, such as fish, eggs, vegetables, and fruits that could be mixed with either dairy products or meat.

The Jews of Polotsk tried to make money, or "chased after *parnosseh*" as they called it, all week in order to provide for the Sabbath. Shops and markets closed early on Friday afternoon, and traveling peddlers, craftsmen, and merchants made an effort to reach home by sundown. From sundown Friday until sundown Saturday, the climactic day of the week was spent quietly in devotion to God. Jews shared a sense of joy as they wished each other "Good Sabbath" and appeared in their best clothes to eat their best meal of the week. Then, more than at any other time, there was the feeling that "it is good to be a Jew."

The men and boys of the shtetl worshiped together in the synagogue at sundown on Friday, and again on Saturday morning when the women often accompanied them.

Blessing the wine and bread by the light of Sabbath candles.

Women sat apart from the men in the synagogue, as they did at weddings and other social functions. Since girls studied only a little Hebrew, few girls or women understood the Hebrew service. At the eastern wall of the synagogue, where the Ark containing the Torah was kept, the learned men, who were the leaders of the shtetl, had their seats of honor.

The various synagogues were the most important places in the shtetl. Jewish leaders met in them to work out shtetl affairs and pass resolutions, and ordinary Jews gathered there after work to rest and chat. Charitable organizations collected donations in the synagogues and used the funds to take care of the sick, lend money to the needy, educate poor boys, and give dowries to orphaned girls. A number of men could always be found in a synagogue studying from the Hebrew books and swaying back and forth in the customary manner as they chanted passages aloud.

Jewish craftsmen and traders who took the train from Polotsk to Vitebsk or on to Vilna to do business or visit relatives saw that not all Jews followed tradition so closely. In the bigger cities of the Pale, they encountered Jews who wore modern European suits with short coats and pressed trousers, who trimmed their beards and cut off their earlocks, who went to Russian schools and spoke Russian instead of Yiddish. When away from Polotsk, craftsmen and traders might clip their own beards and earlocks, remove their long, cumbersome caftans, and travel on the Sabbath, which the law forbade. For them, times were changing. And gradually some of the changes spread to Polotsk and to smaller communities.

WORK AND STUDY

Everyone in the shtetl had to work hard to survive. The self-employed tailor started as early and worked as late as possible at his sewing machine with his wife and daughters helping him. The apprentice labored at least ten hours a day for a master artisan. The peddler, the blacksmith, the shoemaker, and dealers of all kinds often took the train from one shtetl to another in search of parnosseh, since there was not enough in Polotsk for everyone. So few Jews were able to support themselves at a single occupation that many had several, and others shifted desperately from job to job. There was a familiar saying that "the best cobbler of all the tailors is Yankl, the baker." [2]

Regardless of how many trades a man followed or how many people in the family worked, the income was invariably scant. Throughout the week, most families lived on dark rye bread and potatoes with a bit of salt herring or cheese when they could afford it. Even though all members of the family pooled their earnings, they could barely scrape together enough to buy the white bread and fish desired for the Sabbath each week. If a family could not afford a proper meal on Friday night, they were really poor.

The poverty of the Jews resulted not only from the restrictions on where they could live and what sort of work they could do, but also from the endless taxes that they had to pay to the central government and to the town. Like everyone else in Russia, the Jews were taxed on their houses, on their businesses, and on their profits. Everyone paid taxes on candles, yeast, tobacco, and cigarettes. The meat tax for Jews included not only a tax on each pound of meat sold, but also on each animal slaughtered.

> Everyone in the shtetl hated the tax collector. . . . If you didn't have any money to pay your taxes, he took away your candlesticks, your pillows, or your samovar [a Russian urn for making tea].[3]

Serving for four years in the Russian army from the age of twenty-one was another government requirement that placed a heavy burden on the Jews. Jews dreaded the harsh treatment by gentile officers. Low army pay meant that a young man's wife and children suffered when he was away from home, and their business might be ruined by his absence. Worst of all, the army forced Jews to shave their beards, eat food that was not kosher, and drill with guns on the Sabbath. They could not pray each day in the synagogue, and those who tried to pray privately were insulted by gentile officers.

A heavy fine awaited all who evaded military service, but rich Jews could bribe the conscription officers to keep their sons out of the army. The poor might cut off a finger or intentionally injure an arm or leg, an ear or eye, since such damage would cause them to fail the physical examination.

Whether a Jew was a traveling merchant who shipped grain and lumber long distances or a humble tinker who spent his days mending samovars and stoves in a corner of his own home, he longed for his son to become a scholar, the noblest career among Jews, and the one at the top of the status scale. A man stood higher in status if he worked for himself, rather than for someone else. If he were a storekeeper, it was better that he sold woolens than groceries. A salesman had more status than an artisan, for a salesman used his brain and an artisan his hands. No Jew would become a domestic servant if he or she could possibly avoid it, since this was one occupation that was considered shameful.

Rabbis were the most respected men in Polotsk. A rabbi spent his days reading the sacred books so he could advise the Jews of the shtetl whenever they were in doubt about anything. He told a housewife whether or not the chicken she had bought was kosher; he advised a father about a betrothal for his daughter, or a shopkeeper about a business deal; and he mediated disputes between Jews.

Rich or poor, Jews studied the holy books as they had for centuries, even if they could spare only an hour or two a day for reading. They studied primarily to learn the commandments of the Bible that they had to obey to be good Jews. In Russia, where fewer than five percent of the people were literate, nearly every Jew knew how to read either Hebrew or Yiddish.

Somewhere between the ages of three and five, a boy began going to a *cheder*, a one-room school, where he learned to read Hebrew. Most boys stayed on until thirteen, the age of their bar mitzvah, when they assumed the full religious responsibilities of men. Sitting on rough wooden benches beside a table in the teacher's home, fifteen to twenty boys of varying ages repeated over and over again the unfamiliar Hebrew words of the Bible for ten to twelve hours a day. Later they would understand the meaning. Each studied at his own pace, rocking

A scholar works carefully as he inscribes a sacred book.

back and forth as he chanted his lesson aloud. The teacher moved from group to group, listening to boys recite and thrashing any who misbehaved. While beginners intoned the alphabet or learned the prayers, the older boys translated parts of the Torah into Yiddish, or discussed sections of the Talmud. Though everyone raised his voice just as loudly as he could, each managed to concentrate on his own lesson. A gentile teacher came in to instruct the boys in the arithmetic and Russian that the government required.

At the cheder, a boy studied the Hebrew that his father

and grandfather had studied before him, and nothing mattered more to his parents. At home, the schoolboy saw his father reading the Torah or the Talmud in his free time. His mother, who managed the budget, would reduce food costs to a minimum and even pawn her Sabbath candlesticks and treasured pearls, in order to pay her son's tuition fee.

Once a boy began going to school, he had little time to play games. Besides, his parents told him that it was "un-Jewish" to whistle, play with toys, shout, or fight. A father, catching his son at play, would admonish him:

> What? Eight years old and you still want to play around? Are you a heathen? A lad like you should be deep in the Talmud. A lad like you should be studying, not day-dreaming, not skipping about like a goat, as if he hadn't a care in the world! [4]

A boy who was bright and ambitious was sent from the cheder to the *yeshiva*, the most advanced Hebrew school. Here the hours were even longer, with yeshiva students working from daybreak until long past midnight, exhaustively poring over the Talmud in one of the synagogues.

Girls, by comparison, had little schooling. During their several terms at a girls' cheder, they learned enough to read the Yiddish translation of the Bible and to write letters. They also learned to read a few prayers in Hebrew, following the meaning with the help of the Yiddish translation. A girl's real education came at home, where her mother taught her how to bake and cook, sew and embroider, and generally manage a kosher household.

It was assumed that all girls would marry; not to was considered the greatest misfortune. Arranged marriage, negotiated by the parents through a matchmaker, was the tradition of the shtetl, though a modern daughter—a girl who had heard how things were done in Vitebsk or Vilna—might tell her father the name of the boy whom she wanted to marry. Parents looked for a son-in-law whose wealth, learning, and family background were similar to their own, but the better the dowry they could offer for their daughter, the better the husband they could

Under a wedding canopy, a bride and groom face a rabbi.

hope to win. A tailor, for example, could not expect to marry his daughter to the son of a shopkeeper unless he provided her with much more than the poor girl's dowry of a pair of pillows, bedding, a white tablecloth, tableware, and candlesticks. A father considered a scholar the most desirable match for his daughter. People said that "a boy stuffed with learning was worth more than a girl stuffed with bank notes." [5] A girl's father might even support her and her husband until the son-in-law completed his education.

After a couple married, they began to raise a large family, for the first commandment in the Torah told them to "be fruitful and multiply." Parents wanted sons more than daughters, for a boy could raise his status through study and make a good marriage. Furthermore, a son would say *kaddish,* the prayer of mourning for his parents after their death; it was considered a tragedy to have no son to say kaddish. Although daughters were as much beloved as sons, they required dowries and there was a saying, "many daughters, many troubles; many sons, many honors." [6]

DISTRUST AND FEAR

The Jews and the gentile peasants of Polotsk met in the market place, and both drew their livelihood from it. The peasant sold the eggs and potatoes, grain, livestock, fruit, and vegetables from his farm to the Jew; the Jew depended on the peasant to buy the shoes, shirts, lamps, fuel, and dry goods that he made or imported from the city. Jewish women, who came to buy and sell, bargained vivaciously in a combination of Yiddish and Russian.

They wore rumpled cotton dresses with shawls over their shoulders. The baggy trousers of the Jewish men were stuffed into the same wrinkled high boots that the peasants wore, but these could hardly be seen under their caftans.

If anything, the Russian peasants were more impoverished than the Jews. Their miserable thatched hovels housed both family and animals. Desperate for more land, they talked among themselves of seizing some of the aristocrats' estates. The peasants raised so little on their tiny plots that their families lived on the edge of starvation, eating mainly cabbage soup and black bread. Most of the coins they earned by selling farm produce to the Jews quickly left their hands as tax payments to the government.

Much of the time, the Jews and gentiles of Polotsk, who depended on each other's business, lived on friendly enough terms. Yet there was an underlying fear and distrust between them. They inhabited different streets of town and did not understand each other's religion, festivals, language, or ways of thought. The gentiles accused the Jews of cheating them, even though haggling for the best deal was the accepted custom of the market place. And the Jews lived in fear that their businesses might be ruined in a pogrom.

Tension between peasants and Jews was further aggravated by the government under Tsar Nicholas II, which sought to stave off a revolt of the discontented peasants by convincing them that it was the Jews, not the government, who were responsible for their distress. In the Russian high school of Polotsk, gentile boys, and the few

Jewish boys that the government allowed to attend, were taught that Jewish bankers, moneylenders, and merchants took too much money from their gentile customers. A Russian-language newspaper, sold in Polotsk to the few literate gentiles, might slyly encourage its readers to ridicule the Jews about their food, their clothes, their Sabbath, and their ancient Hebrew language.

The Russian police in Pale towns stood by quietly during murderous riots directed against Jews. Perhaps a government officer from St. Petersburg would start a rumor that a Jew had murdered a Christian; or at Easter time, the priests would repeat the cry that the Jews had crucified Jesus Christ. Angry peasants would set out to kill as many Jews as they could. Somehow, Polotsk escaped having any pogroms, perhaps because the Jews there lived on friendlier terms with the peasants than Jews in other towns did.

On many occasions, though, refugees fleeing a pogrom or ordered out of their town by the tsar's police would limp into Polotsk carrying the only possessions they had salvaged—a few feather pillows, a pair of precious candlesticks, some books and clothing. They told horrible stories about peasants, drunk with vodka, attacking Jews, and the police not intervening until the damage was done. The peasants, the refugees said, broke windows and furniture, smashed household utensils and dishes, ripped open pillows and featherbeds, sending the contents swirling in the streets. They burst into shops, scattered the wares, poured kerosene over them, and set them on fire. Even synagogues were not spared the lash of attackers who desecrated buildings and ripped Torah scrolls to

Police watch as Jews are assaulted during a pogrom in Kiev.

shreds. Gentiles cut off an earlock here, forcibly shortened a caftan there, cruelly beat some Jews with clubs or scythes, and savagely murdered others.

Some of the refugees found new homes and jobs in Polotsk or a nearby town, but others who had seen their homes destroyed and their businesses ruined, gave up the struggle for parnosseh in Russia. They raised the cry: "To America." America was simply a name, not a place that these Jews knew much about. But it represented a chance to earn a "more beautiful parnosseh" in safety, to worship without ridicule, and to have civil rights. Not many Jews from Polotsk joined the refugees on their journey from the Pale to the unknown. They chose to stay in a dangerous but known land where they trusted, if trouble came, they would not starve or die alone. Encouraged by a Zionist organization, some probably awaited the day when Jews could raise enough money to emigrate to Palestine and establish a self-governing community in the land they believed God had promised to the Jews. Others hoped that the departure of some tailors, shoemakers, and shopkeepers from Polotsk would leave more business for those who stayed behind. They also hoped that, in time, a revolutionary movement to overthrow the tsar would succeed. Such a movement was under way.

Revolutionary activity climbed to a peak in 1904 and 1905 when Russia's disastrous defeats in a war with Japan made the people of the Russian Empire more aware than ever of the corruption and inefficiency of high government officials. A ferment of disorder swept through Russia. Terrorists threw bombs, scuffled with police, and assassinated government officials, especially in the large cities. Soldiers revolted against their officers, and peasants burned landlords' houses. There were many Jews among the leaders of this revolution.

Almost every Jew in Polotsk heard about the agitation in the cities by reading the Yiddish leaflets and newspapers circulated throughout the Pale by the Bund. This was an organization of Jewish workers led by youths who had studied at universities in industrialized nations and who wanted to improve working conditions in Russia and end all discriminatory anti-Jewish laws. Some Jews in Polotsk went to secret Bund meetings, where revolutionaries denounced tsarist tyranny and described street demonstrations, boycotts, and strikes that had taken place in the big cities.

Bund leaders together with gentiles organized a general strike that brought the 1904-05 revolution to its climax. All over Russia, railroad workers stopped working, and shipyard workers, factory hands, miners, shopkeepers, and bankers followed their lead. Teachers refused to teach and ballet dancers to dance. With his country paralysed, Tsar Nicholas II reluctantly promised to let the people have a representative assembly to advise him in making laws. But the tsar only partly kept his promise, and after a few months the revolution collapsed. Then the tsar blamed the whole disturbance on the Jews and urged his subjects to protest against the "Jewish revolution."

Hundreds of Jews were murdered and thousands badly beaten in the rash of pogroms that followed. Still more Jews died of hunger or saw their businesses ruined. As before, there was no pogrom in Polotsk, but people there, hearing descriptions of pogroms elsewhere, lived in more fear than ever that one might erupt in their town. Now that the revolution had failed, Jews in Polotsk and throughout the Pale saw no hope for an end to their oppression.

AMERICA: THE PROMISED LAND

Contrary to expectations, the departure of some Jews from Polotsk had not made the search for parnosseh there any easier. Craftsmen and shopkeepers who stayed behind found they had fewer customers to buy their goods. In addition to the Jews who had left, many gentile peasants had moved to larger cities to work in factories.

To make matters worse, Jewish craftsmen found that they could no longer compete with the increasing number of factory-made products. One small business after another failed and all hope of earning a decent livelihood vanished. The dream of finding a better parnosseh in America replaced it. Hesitation about leaving the familiar streets of Polotsk was overcome by the terrorism of pogroms. For innumerable Russian Jews, America took on the image of the Promised Land.

> Businessmen talked of it over their accounts; the market women made up their quarrels that they might discuss it from stall to stall; people who had relatives in the famous land went around reading their letters for the enlightenment of less fortunate folks; the one letter-carrier informed the public how many letters arrived from America and who were the recipients; children played at emigration; old folks shook their sage heads over the evening fire, and prophesied no good for those who braved the terrors of the sea and the foreign goal beyond it. [7]

German steamship companies advertised cheap transatlantic passage, and letters from America reported that America needed laborers and paid them well. According to these letters, from the moment they arrived Jewish newcomers would have as many rights as everyone else; they could live where they pleased and do whatever work they wanted with hope of saving enough money to bring friends and relatives across; there was free education and no compulsory military service; and they need not fear persecution for their religious customs.

Family after family in Polotsk and throughout the Pale resolved to begin life over again in the New World. They dismantled their homes, selling furniture, books, and boxes of belongings, but they kept their Bibles and prayerbooks, the precious bedding which was an important part of every dowry, their samovars, and some pots and pans. Having been warned of border guards and ticket agents who might swindle them, they sewed into the linings of their jackets the few rubles they had managed to save or the dollars sent to them from America.

On the day of a family's departure, it seemed that over half the town appeared at the railroad station to wish them a good journey. Uncertainty, desolation, and homesickness filled the hearts of the emigrants as their train pulled out of the station, carrying them away from the only life they had ever known. They were embarking on an enormous journey with very little experience in traveling, not enough money, no knowledge of the conditions, customs, and language of the place to which they were going, and only a vague idea of their route, future plans, and final destination. But the changing world of the shtetl had helped prepare them for the modern country to which they were going.

Trains, thickly packed with refugees, moved across western Russia and Germany to the ports of Hamburg and Bremen where the emigrants would board a ship. Jews who were evading conscription or who had been leaders of the anti-tsarist movement had no passports and were forced to steal through the woods across the border and out of Russia. The Jews who left Polotsk were part of a migration of nearly two million Jews from eastern Europe between 1881 and 1914. Some were going to Canada and Argentina, a few to Palestine and various other countries, but most of them were going to New York. And in New York the majority of them remained, though some built synagogues along the Atlantic coast and in the Middle West, while others carried copies of the Torah to the Pacific coast.

FROM PEONAGE

Hacienda Buenavista, Mexico, 1920's

TO FIELDS AND KITCHENS

Even before dawn, the sound of women slapping tortillas could be heard in each of the villages on the lands of Hacienda Buenavista. Women got up first to make the thin flat corncakes that their husbands and sons ate for breakfast and carried to the fields for lunch. After softening the corn kernels in warm lime water and boiling them in an earthenware pot to remove their husks, a woman rubbed the pulp against a grinding stone with a second stone to smooth it into dough. She rolled a bit of dough into a ball, slapped it quickly into a pancake shape, and threw it down on the earthen or iron griddle set over a charcoal fire. The hearth at which she knelt consisted simply of three stones to support the griddle. She made at least a hundred tortillas every morning and more later. Each working man in the family ate about twenty-five a day, the women of the household ate at least a dozen apiece, and the small children somewhat fewer.